Depression

CW00530392

In recent years there has been an increase in research into childhood depression, and it is now recognised that depression can severely impair young people in many aspects of their life, school, peer and social relationships, and frequently persists into adulthood.

Depression: Cognitive Behaviour Therapy with Children and Young People provides an accessible guide to recognising and treating depression in young people. Based on a successful manual developed for research trials, this book presents an overview of a cognitive behavioural model for working with this age group, as well as practical ideas about how to start therapy. Topics covered include:

- engaging young people
- setting goals for therapy
- cognitive behaviour assessment and formulation
- solutions for problems practitioners may face
- encouraging parents and agencies to support therapy.

Depression includes case examples and practical tips to prepare the practitioner for working with young people. Information is presented in a readable and practical style making this book ideal for professionals working in child and adolescent mental health services, as well as those in training. It will also be a useful guide for people working in community services for children and young people.

Online resources:
This book contains worksheets that can be downloaded free of charge to purchasers of the print version. Please visit the website www.routledge mentalhealth.com/cbt-with-children to find out more about this facility.

Chrissie Verduyn is Director of Clinical Psychology and Joint Clinical Director, Manchester and Salford CAMHS.

Julia Rogers is a Case Manager at Bolton CAMHS.

Alison Wood is a Consultant Child and Adolescent Psychiatrist at Pine Lodge Young People's Centre, Chester.

CBT with Children, Adolescents and Families
Series editor: Paul Stallard

"The *CBT with Children, Adolescents and Families* series, edited by Professor Paul Stallard and written by a team of international experts, meets the growing need for evidence-based treatment manuals to address prevalent psychological problems in young people. These authoritative, yet practical books will be of interest to all professionals who work in the field of child and adolescent mental health." – *Alan Carr, Professor of Clinical Psychology, University College Dublin, Ireland*

Cognitive behaviour therapy (CBT) is now the predominant treatment approach in both the NHS and private practice and is increasingly used by a range of mental health professionals.

The *CBT with Children, Adolescents and Families* series provides comprehensive, practical guidance for using CBT when dealing with a variety of common child and adolescent problems, as well as related family issues. The demand for therapy and counselling for children and adolescents is rapidly expanding, and early intervention in family and school settings is increasingly seen as effective and essential. In this series leading authorities in their respective fields provide detailed advice on methods of achieving this.

Each book in this series focuses on one particular problem and guides the professional from initial assessment through to techniques, common problems and future issues. Written especially for the clinician, each title includes summaries of key points, clinical examples, and worksheets to use with children and young people.

Titles in this series:

Depression

Cognitive Behaviour Therapy with Children and Young People

Chrissie Verduyn, Julia Rogers and Alison Wood

Routledge
Taylor & Francis Group

LONDON AND NEW YORK

First published 2009
by Routledge
27 Church Road, Hove, East Sussex BN3 2FA

Simultaneously published in the USA and Canada
by Routledge
270 Madison Avenue, New York, NY 10016

Routledge is an imprint of the Taylor & Francis Group, an informa business

Typeset in Times by RefineCatch Ltd, Bungay, Suffolk
Printed and bound in Great Britain by TJ International Ltd, Padstow, Cornwall
Paperback cover design by Andy Ward

This publication has been produced with paper manufactured to strict
environmental standards and with pulp derived from sustainable forests.

British Library Cataloguing in Publication Data
A catalogue record for this book is available from the British Library

Library of Congress Cataloging-in-Publication Data
Verduyn, Chrissie.
    Depression : cognitive behaviour therapy with children and young people /
Chrissie Verduyn, Julia Rogers, and Alison Wood.
        p. ; cm.
    Includes bibliographical references and index.
    1. Depression in children.   2. Depression in adolescence.   3. Cognitive therapy
for children.   4. Cognitive therapy for teenagers.   I. Rogers, Julia, 1962–
II. Wood, Alison, 1960–   III. Title.
    [DNLM: 1. Depression–therapy.   2. Adolescent.   3. Child.   4. Cognitive
Therapy–methods. WM 171 V487d 2009]
    RJ506.D4V47 2009
    618.85′27–dc22

                                                                            2008041900

ISBN: 978-0-415-39977-7 (hbk)
ISBN: 978-0-415-39978-4 (pbk)

Dedication

This book is dedicated to Professor Richard Harrington. Dick worked as professor of child and adolescent psychiatry in Manchester from 1997 until his untimely death in 2007. Dick inspired major clinical research projects in Manchester and his special interest was in the treatment of adolescent depressive disorders. Dick's undaunting enthusiasm, creativity and empowerment of others will always be remembered.

Contents

1

Depression in adolescence

Until the 1970s it was generally believed that depressive disorders as seen in adults were rare in childhood. Depressive symptoms were considered a normal part of adolescence. Mood swings, low mood and irritability were seen as the consequences of developmental changes involved in the onset of puberty and adjusting to increasing independence and role changes. Studies in the 1970s and 1980s (Puig-Antich, 1982; Pearce, 1978; Weinberg et al., 1973) showed that depressive disorders occurred before adulthood. It is now recognised that depression can severely impair a young person in many important aspects of their life, school, peer and social relationships, and also will frequently persist into adulthood. In recent years there has been a significant increase in research activity in the area of depression in children and young people but still there are gaps in knowledge compared with the work on adults. The focus of research has moved away from the nature of depression in young people to recognition of the need for better identification of symptoms, referral on to appropriate services and delivering effective treatments.

In clinical use, the term depression is used to describe a cluster of symptoms involving significant changes in mood, in thinking and in activity. These symptoms persist and result in changes in personal and social functioning over a period of at least 2 weeks. Depressed mood may be accompanied by tearfulness and includes sadness and/or irritability with a loss of enjoyment of everyday activities. Children appear unhappy and may report feeling hopeless, helpless and miserable. Cognitive changes can include changes in ability to concentrate and attend to school work. Feelings of worthlessness, self-blame and a general lack of confidence are often present. In severe depression the young person may feel guilty and personally responsible for any past problems. This can be associated with suicidal ideas.

There may be changes in sleeping, eating, energy levels and motivation. Sleep problems may occur in a number of different ways but will involve a change from the young person's normal pattern. There may be increased sleeping, early morning wakening or insomnia. Appetite may increase, with comfort eating, or decrease. Weight loss or failure to gain weight may be noted.

> *Ella, age 14, lives with her mother and two older brothers. She has some good friends whom she has known since they started nursery together. She enjoys listening to music, chatting online, shopping, going to the cinema or hanging around in the local park with friends at the weekend. Things at home are fine. Her mother works full time in an office. She feels low from time to time and does not go out much. Ella and her brothers see their father every week. He lives about 2 miles away. He and their mother separated 4 years ago and he has a new partner and baby. The first thing anyone noticed was that Ella had become bad-tempered. She would get annoyed if her friends were late or had forgotten to do something. She had been in fights with another group of girls in school and the school contacted her mother. She was getting into trouble in class and was not doing her school work and homework. She didn't want to go to school in the mornings and her friends stopped waiting for her at the bus stop. At home her mother had to get on to her about doing anything to help. When she was in she disappeared to her room and avoided being around at mealtimes. Ella could not talk to anyone about feeling that everything she did was bad or wrong or pointless and that no one liked or had ever cared about her. She found it hard to think straight at all.*
>
> *A couple of months after the depression started Ella had an argument with a friend at school and walked out. The school phoned her mother and she and Ella had a major row. Ella felt completely hopeless and could see no future. She felt that she was just a problem making everyone's life more difficult. She took an overdose of her mother's tablets. An hour later she felt sick, panicked and went round to a friend's house and told her what she had done. At the hospital she had to stay overnight for treatment. On the following day she saw one of the Child and Adolescent Mental Health Service (CAMHS) team, who also met her mother and talked to her head of year, with her mother's agreement. The CAMHS worker helped her understand that she was depressed.*

The presentation of a depressive disorder depends on the developmental stage of the young person. The ability to communicate about experiences can vary widely between young people. Cognitive development influences the symptom profile. For example, feelings of guilt, existential thinking, nihilism and morbid introspection are usually only described by older, more mature adolescents. Younger adolescents may show more dependent behaviour with parents than usual.

The origins of the depressive disorder and the particular way it presents itself will vary according to the circumstances of the individual but research has highlighted the following main areas of difficulty.

Main features of depression in adolescents

Mood changes:

- sadness, misery
- irritability.

Negative styles of thinking:

- low self-esteem
- feelings of helplessness and hopelessness
- suicidal thinking.

Difficulties with social relationships:

- social withdrawal
- social skills problems
- social problem-solving difficulties.

Physical symptoms of depression:

- sleep disturbance
- appetite disturbance
- inactivity
- loss of interest, apathy.

The effects of depression are wide ranging, and involve changes in the young person's behaviour, feelings and thoughts. Commonly a vicious circle is created, in which symptoms of depression enhance themselves. For example, inactivity leads to disturbed sleep and to increased time for worrying, both of which increase the symptom of low mood, which in turn leads to further inactivity. Lack of sleep and poor concentration can lead to problems with schoolwork and an increasing sense of failure. As for Ella, irritability and sensitivity can lead to arguments and difficulties in relationships which escalate and prove to the young person that they are hopeless, worthless and that no one cares about them.

Diagnosis of depression

It is now generally accepted that depressive disorders occur in children and adolescents and that these can be diagnosed according to adult criteria (Harrington and Wood, 1995). The two international diagnostic systems, Diagnostic and Statistical Manual of Mental Disorders (DSM-IV; American Psychiatric Association, 1994) and International Classification of Diseases

(ICD-10; World Health Organization, 1993) both categorise depression as mild, moderate and severe. ICD-10 puts the emphasis on symptoms whereas DSM-IV considers symptoms and functional impairment.

Both ICD-10 and DSM-IV require that symptoms be present for at least 2 weeks. ICD-10 describes depressive episodes as mild (F32.0); moderate (F32.1) and severe (F32.2 and F32.3). For each, at least two of the most typical symptoms (depressed mood, loss of interest and enjoyment, increased fatiguability) are required with the presence of at least three additional symptoms for moderate, and at least four, all of severe intensity, to be present for severe depression. Additional symptoms that must be present nearly every day are weight or appetite loss, sleep disturbance, observed restlessness or being slowed down, feelings of worthlessness, impaired concentration and morbid thinking or suicidal ideation. ICD-10 also includes a category for psychotic symptoms (F32.3).

DSM-IV requires the presence of five or more symptoms that result in significant distress or impairment in social, occupational or other important areas of functioning. In younger children psychosomatic symptoms such as abdominal pain or headaches may be prominent as well as separation anxiety, school refusal or failure to progress academically. In older children irritability, anxiety, motor agitation and social withdrawal feature more.

It appears that depressive disorder for children is different from that for adolescents. Children are more likely to have depression with another disorder (Alpert *et al.*, 1999) and the diagnosis is commonly associated with major family dysfunction (Harrington *et al.*, 1997).

It is now recognised that young people presenting with symptoms of depression that do not meet the threshold for diagnosis are vulnerable to developing full-blown depressive disorders. These young people with 'subthreshold' depression are more likely to become depressed than the general population (Costello *et al.*, 1999). Depression is often encountered in young people following traumatic events such as assault or rape, where there are chronic family problems, where there is drug or alcohol misuse, aggressive behaviour or chronic school attendance problems.

> Severity of depression is rated according to the number of symptoms present and degree of impairment in everyday life. Symptoms vary with age. Depressive symptoms commonly exacerbate life problems in a vicious cycle.

Multiple problems (co-morbidity)

In specialist mental health services depression is rarely seen in isolation. Concurrent symptoms of behaviour problems or anxiety will be present in almost all cases and between 50% and 80% of depressed young people will also meet criteria for another disorder. About 25% will have conduct or oppositional defiant disorder and a similar figure for anxiety disorder (Goodyer and Cooper, 1993; Angold and Costello, 1995). Other problems may have been present for several years. It may appear that the challenges presented by coping with difficulties in childhood become manifest as low self-esteem as the young person enters adolescence and is more acutely aware of their problems. The presence of multiple problems challenges successful intervention.

Depression can also be associated with physical illness such as diabetes, asthma or rheumatoid arthritis.

Some depressed young people use alcohol or drugs in an attempt to feel better. The after effects may compound difficulties for instance drugs such as cocaine may cause an irritable, depressed state (Barker, 2004).

> Co-morbidity with other emotional and conduct disorders is common.

Suicidality and self-harm

Suicide or suicidal behaviour is associated with depressive disorders in adolescents (Kerfoot *et al.*, 1996). Andrews and Lewinsohn (1992) found that adolescents who had deliberately self-harmed were 3–18 times more likely to be depressed than a control group. Pfeffer *et al.* (1993) found that non-depressed self-harmers had less suicidal ideation and less risk of future problems than the depressed group. Weissman *et al.* (1999) found that 7% of adolescents who developed a depressive disorder are at risk of committing suicide in their young adult years. Boys were more at risk of suicidal behaviour especially if they have a conduct disorder and alcohol or substance misuse (Shaffer and Craft, 1999). It is important for clinicians to enquire routinely about suicidal thoughts and self-harm and assess risk (see Chapter 10 for management of self-harm).

> There is a strong relationship between depression and self-harm.

How common is depression?

Adolescent depressive disorder is not uncommon. Fleming *et al.* (1989) reviewed early studies and found the level of prevalence ranged from 1% to

6%. More recent studies have confirmed this. In a national survey of children's mental health (Meltzer *et al.*, 2000), 4% of 5 to 15-year-olds had an emotional disorder (anxiety and depression). Most studies have found that depressive disorder is much more common in adolescents than pre-adolescents (Olsson and Van Knorring, 1999; Angold *et al.*, 1998a). Meltzer and colleagues found that participants were 8.5 times more likely to have depression at age 11 to 15 compared to age 5 to 10.

Studies consistently show increased prevalence associated with social disadvantage including living with a lone parent, parental unemployment and parents scoring highly on questionnaires suggesting emotional disorder (Hill, 1995; Melzer *et al.*, 2000; Corcoran and Franklin, 2002; Myers, 2000).

Evidence from several studies suggests that ethnicity does not have a significant impact on the risk of adolescent major depression after socio-demographic adjustments are made (Doi *et al.*, 2001; Chen *et al.*, 1998; Roberts *et al.*, 1997).

Studies have estimated that as many as 75% of children and adolescents with a clinically identifiable mood disorder are untreated in the community (Andrews *et al.*, 2002; Coyle *et al.*, 2003).

> Between 1% and 6% of children will suffer from depression with rates increasing during adolescence.

Causes and factors in the development of depression

A substantial majority of young people experience depression in the context of long standing family and social difficulties, some with a clear precipitating life event and others with a slow deterioration in coping socially and in the family. In adulthood similar multiple pathways to depression have been described (Kendler *et al.*, 2002).

It is most likely that the aetiology of adolescent, as for adult, depressive disorder is multifactorial. Theoretical models of depression include biochemical, genetic, psycho-social, and socio-economic frameworks. Some are summarised below.

Biochemical theories, such as the monoamine hypothesis, describe how underactivity in brain amine systems causes depression. Carlson and Garber (1986) proposed that too little serotonergic activity resulted in agitated depression and too little noradrenergic activity results in lethargic depression. This is discussed further in relation to use of medication in treatment of depression (see page 8).

Genetic studies have indicated that genetic predisposition plays a more significant role in bipolar disorder than in unipolar depression (Kendler *et al.*, 1995).

Children who develop major depression are more likely to have a family history of the disorder, often a parent who suffered depression in adolescence. This is unlikely to be owing to genetic influences alone (Harrington *et al.*, 1997). Environmental and familial factors play a significant role in the aetiology of adolescent depression. Harrington (1994, 1999) argued that family factors are more widespread than a genetic factor in the development of adolescent depression. Parental depression can impact directly on the child's early environment as symptoms may cause impaired parenting skills, lack of warmth or hostility to the child (Goodman and Gotlib, 1999). Parental depression is associated with marital discord (Quinton and Rutter, 1985). Asarnow *et al.* (1988) found that young people who had inpatient treatment for depression had worse outcomes if discharged to families with high levels of expressed emotion than those with a less critical family.

Harrington (1999) discussed the importance of bi-directional influences. Children with problems are a stress to their parents. There may be depressed thinking about their competence as parents. Negative cycles of interactions can develop and exacerbate parental depression (Hammen, 1991).

The social environment outside the family may also be influential on the development of depression in adolescents. Acute life events, including problems with peers and bullying may contribute directly (Harrington, 1992). Maternal depression is associated with social deprivation (Fergusson *et al.*, 1995). Parental unemployment, poor housing, poor support networks and poor standards of living are all associated with increased risk of psychological disorders (Mental Health Foundation, 1999).

Once a young person is depressed, environmental factors associated with development of the disorder such as family relationship problems or school failure may then escalate and impair chances of successful recovery.

> Biochemical, genetic, psycho-social and socio-economic influences have been identified as contributing factors to the development of depression.

Course of depression

The majority of young people with a depressive episode will recover. Around 10% of depressed young people will recover within 3 months and a further 40% within the first year. At 2 years about 20% remain depressed (Harrington and Dubicka, 2001; Goodyer *et al.*, 2003). About 30% of individuals will have a further episode within 5 years (Fombonne *et al.*, 2001).

Longer term, depressed young people are likely to suffer from depression in adulthood. Harrington *et al.* (1991) in a follow-up study found that depressed young people had four times more episodes than the non-depressed group after the age 17 years.

Characteristics of the original depressive episode can, in part, predict future risks. Children who are older at first episode are more likely than younger children to experience depression in adulthood. Relapses may be because of environmental factors (Asarnow *et al.*, 1988) or parental depression (Radke-Yarrow *et al.*, 1992; Hammen, 1991). Pfeffer *et al.* (1991) found that those who attempted suicide, when compared with a control group, were ten times more likely to have a depressive disorder within the 8 year follow-up. Fombonne *et al.* (2001) quoted rates of attempted suicide of 44% and completed suicide of 2.5% at 20-year follow-up. A small number of individuals will go on to develop bipolar affective disorder.

Depressive disorders can affect young people's functioning after the mood disorder is resolved. There is increased risk of illness, interpersonal problems, suicidal behaviour and substance misuse (Birmaher *et al.*, 1998; Ryan *et al.*, 1987; Weissman *et al.*, 1999).

> The majority of children with depression will recover although 1 in 5 will still be depressed 2 years after onset. Longer term, young people who have been depressed are much more likely than those who have not to experience depression as adults.

Treatments for depression

Young people's rights and the treatment context

In the UK, it is good practice and a legal requirement for young people themselves to provide consent to treatment if they have sufficient understanding to fully understand what is involved. They have a right to confidentiality in health care in their own right which can only be breached by health professionals if there are justifiable concerns about the young person's welfare for instance risk of self-harm. In practice, parents or legal guardians are frequently responsible for supporting young people in seeking access to mental health services. Working with parents and carers is a crucial element of working with all aspects of a young person's problems and as such their consent and contribution will also be important.

> Young people should provide consent to treatment in their own right.

Medication

The monoamine hypothesis proposed that depression can result from underactivity of monoamine neurotransmitter systems in the brain (Deakin and Crow, 1986). Support for this hypothesis comes from observations that drugs which inhibit monoamine reuptake have an antidepresssant effect. There are three main groups of antidepressant medication which bring this about: tricyclic antidepressants, selective serotonin reuptake inhibitors (SSRIs) and monoamine oxidase inhibitors. In addition, two other groups of medication may be indicated in the management of young people with severe depressive disorders. These are the mood stabilisers and the atypical antipsychotics.

For the UK, the National Institute for Health and Clinical Excellence (NICE) Guideline (2005a) recommends that antidepressant medication should not be used for the initial treatment of children and young people with mild depression. For children with moderate depression, assessment by a child and adolescent mental health specialist and the offer of psychological interventions are regarded as first-line treatment. Antidepressant medication, in combination with psychological interventions is recommended if there is no response. The guideline recommended fluoxetine (an SSRI) as the medication of choice. For young people with psychotic depression, augmenting treatment with antipsychotic medication should be considered. Prescription of medication should occur only following assessment by a child and adolescent psychiatrist.

Selective serotonin reuptake inhibitors (SSRIs)

The five SSRIs are fluoxetine, paroxetine, fluvoxamine, citalopram and sertraline. In the 1990s the SSRI group of antidepressants replaced the tricyclic antidepressants as first-line medication treatment for children and young people suffering from depressive disorders. Evidence accumulated for their benefit in the treatment of various childhood psychiatric disorders and in 2002 Emslie and colleagues (2002) demonstrated the superiority of fluoxetine over placebo in the treatment of depression in children and adolescents. In 2003 a meta-analysis of efficacy and unwanted effects raised doubts about the balance of benefit for these drugs (Khan *et al.*, 2003). Common side effects of SSRIs include nausea, sleep disturbance, agitation, sexual dysfunction and weight gain. Discontinuation of SSRIs with a short half-life, for instance paroxetine, commonly results in a withdrawal syndrome. Concerns were raised specifically regarding paroxetine having the potential for increase in suicidality.

In 2003, paroxetine was withdrawn for use with children and adolescents by the UK Committee for Safety of Medicines and later, in the same year, concerns about the limited evidence base for the effectiveness of SSRIs as a group led to withdrawal of all drugs in this class for use in those under 18 years of age with the exception of fluoxetine.

The debate about the risks and benefits of SSRIs for adolescent depression has continued. A meta-analysis of data submitted to the US Food and Drug Administration submitted for marketing approval of the six most widely prescribed antidepressants between 1987 and 1999 including unpublished data showed that drug-placebo differences in antidepressant efficacy increase as a function of baseline severity but are relatively small even for severely depressed patients (Kirsch *et al.*, 2008). A further meta-analysis of all randomised controlled trials (RCTs) involving depressed young people under the age of 20 generated 29 studies meeting criteria. Meta-analysis showed a modest pooled drug/placebo response rate ratio (RR=1.22, 95% CI 1.15–1.31) with little separation between antidepressants. Fluoxetine emerged as more effective in adolescents. More studies of severely depressed suicidal patients are needed (Tsapakis *et al.*, 2008). These two meta-analyses confirm that there is a place for fluoxetine in severe adolescent depression preferably alongside psychological therapy with close monitoring and further research is required.

Tricyclic antidepressants

A meta-analysis of studies examining the use of tricyclic antidepressants in the treatment of childhood depression confirmed their lack of efficacy with this age group (Hazell *et al.*, 1995). The side effect profile of the tricyclic antidepressants is unacceptable. Common side effects include dry mouth, blurred vision, constipation and sleep disturbance. Cardiotoxicity is a major problem with overdose. There are now no indications for their continuing use in treatment of depressed young people.

Mood stabilisers

This group includes lithium, sodium valproate, carbamazepine and lamotrigine. Lithium has traditionally been the agent of first choice in the treatment of bipolar affective disorder. Much less is known about the use of lithium in children and adolescents but there is some evidence that it is effective (Geller *et al.*, 1998). As lithium requires monitoring of serum levels and has a problematic side effect profile and significant toxicity in overdose, the use of sodium valproate and carbamazepine has increased. Both of these are anticonvulsants but there is substantial evidence that in the long term they operate as mood stabilisers in children and young people. Both have severe side effects. More evidence is needed regarding the benefits of mood stabilisers in children and adolescents.

Atypical antipsychotics

For the treatment of psychotic depression it has been recommended that an atypical antipsychotic such as risperidone, olanzapine or quietapine, is added to an antidepressant in the management plan (Spiker *et al.*, 1985). The side effects of atypical antipsychotics vary. For most young people sedation, weight gain and sleep disturbance may occur.

- Medication is not recommended for the initial treatment of mild depression.

- For moderate depression, medication should be used in combination with psychological treatment.
- Fluoxetine (SSRI) is recommended as the medication of choice.

Psychological treatments

Psychological treatments that have been used to help depressed young people include self-help, individual, family and group treatments based on different theoretical models. Few have been evaluated. The evidence base for cognitive behaviour therapy (CBT) is outlined from p. 23.

In a meta-analysis of all psychological treatments for depression (Weisz *et al.*, 2006) the treatment effects were described as modest compared with outcomes for other disorders, such as anxiety. Watanabe *et al.* (2007) in a further meta-analysis of psychotherapies used a different methodology, including intention-to-treat analyses, and took a clinical perspective on outcomes ('response' was a below threshold score for diagnosis of depression). They reported that psychotherapies, especially CBT, which had the largest body of evidence, and interpersonal therapy (IPT) were more effective than no treatment, waiting list or attention placebo at post-treatment. Effectiveness was greatest for 12–18-year-olds and for those with moderate to severe depression. Treatment effects were no longer evident at follow-up after 6 months, due to improvement in symptoms in untreated groups. Very few studies have included long term follow-up.

Several therapies have been shown to be successful at treatment endpoint. Interpersonal therapy (IPT) was developed as a brief, time-limited psychotherapy for depressed adults in the 1960s. Depression is addressed in the arena of social relationships. The adolescent programme is for 12 sessions including education about depression, relating depression to the social context, clarifying goals and problem areas for change, problem-solving and communication skills work (Fombonne, 1998). The clinician is active in directing sessions and supporting the young person and works in the here-and-now. IPT has been compared to waiting list or standard care controls and shown to increase remission and reduce symptoms (Mufson *et al.*, 1999, 2004; Rossello and Bernal, 1999).

In psychodynamic approaches to therapy the focus is on past experiences with the young person gaining insight and working on issues through the therapeutic relationship. There are no published studies comparing psychodynamic therapy with a no treatment control group. Trowell *et al.* (2007) suggested that individual psychodynamic psychotherapy is as effective as family therapy in treatment of moderate to severe depression. There is inconclusive evidence from the small number of studies examining the effectiveness of family therapy (Brent *et al.*, 1997).

Combinations of medication and psychological treatments

Important recent research has focused on the comparison of antidepressants with psychological treatments and their combination in adolescents. The Treatment for Adolescents with Depression Study (TADS, 2004) in the USA took a very large sample of moderate to severely depressed young people and compared fluoxetine and CBT over 12 weeks with a combination of both and with a placebo (pill). CBT and medication together were found to be more effective than medication alone. Treatment with medication alone was superior to either placebo or CBT alone. Long-term outcomes from this study are continuing to emerge. Results 9 months after the start of treatment demonstrated continuing improvement in the CBT groups, with the CBT alone group showing a comparable response to medication alone. The placebo group ended at 12 weeks. Suicidal ideation decreased with treatment but less with fluoxetine than with combination therapy or with CBT alone (TADS, 2007).

In a study based in primary care within the USA, Clarke *et al.* (2005) compared CBT and SSRIs as a combination with SSRIs alone and found slightly superior outcomes with the combination therapy. However a UK clinic-based multi-site study (Goodyer *et al.*, 2007) found no differences in outcomes between adolescents with moderate to severe depression treated with SSRI alone compared to SSRI and CBT after 12 weeks of treatment or at 28 weeks. By 28 weeks, 57% of the young people were much or very much improved with 20% remaining unimproved. The authors suggest that the sample was probably the most severely impaired in any RCT to date.

- Depression is common and will affect up to 6% of young people at any time.
- Depression is much commoner in adolescents than in younger age groups.
- Depression in adolescence carries a high risk for recurrent depression in adulthood.
- There is considerable co-morbidity with other disorders particularly anxiety and conduct disorder.
- There are multiple pathways to the development of depression with biochemical, genetic, family and environmental factors all likely to contribute.
- Few psychological treatments have been evaluated by randomised controlled trial.
- Medication can play a part in treatment of moderate to severe depression but only fluoxetine is recommended and in combination with psychological treatment.

2

Cognitive behaviour therapy: an introduction and overview

Cognitive behaviour therapy (CBT) is a structured therapy which helps people tackle problems from the perspective of understanding thoughts and beliefs, particularly negative thoughts, and how they link with feelings and behaviour. The psychotherapeutic models were originally established in work with adults.

Cognitive behavioural models of depression

CBT is based on an understanding of the development and experience of symptoms of depression. The cognitive behavioural model is based on the assumption that negative experiences as a child result in negative core schema about oneself. Negative styles of thinking may stem from early childhood experiences, for instance poor relationships at home, criticism, persisting experience of failure at school. These negative experiences may lead to low self-esteem. Later events, such as bereavements, separations or losses in close relationships may then trigger the onset of depression. Negative thoughts and thinking errors affect mood. As mood becomes more depressed, the negative cognitions become more frequent and affect behaviour, thus creating a downward spiral of increasing depression. Figure 2.1 illustrates a cognitive model of depression.

Aaron Beck's model is the best known and most extensively used. Beck's model and theory of depression evolved from systematic clinical observation and experimental testing. There are three main components of Beck's cognitive theory. The first defines schemata as the cognitive structures that organise experience and behaviour. The content of these is represented by beliefs and rules and they determine the content of the thinking, affect and behaviour (Beck, 1990). Schemata are relatively stable cognitive patterns that influence how a person makes sense of themselves and their world.

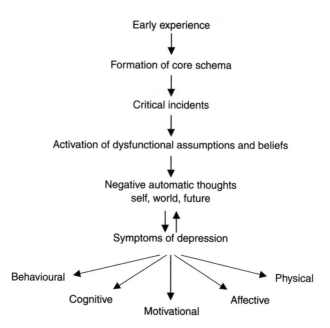

Figure 2.1   A cognitive model of depression

Depressive schemata develop over many years and are activated by a combination of stressful circumstances.

Schemata can be broken down into five different types.

- Control schemata involve self-monitoring, inhibiting, modifying and directing actions.
- Cognitive schemata are concerned with the interpretation of oneself and others.
- Affective schemas generate feelings and emotions.
- Motivational schemata deal with desires and aspirations.
- Instrumental schemata prepare people for action.

Schemata working together create interpretations of situations and produce responses.

Beck *et al.* (1979) described an active processing of information with cognitions resulting from the combination of internal and external stimuli, from interpretation of events. These cognitions are the second main component of Beck's theory; 'negative automatic thoughts' reflect the meaning that people give to themselves, their world, their past and their future. Their content is negative, critical and dysfunctional. The thoughts are automatic in that they seem to come 'out of the blue'. They seem valid to the individual and are accepted without reflection. Their effect is to lower mood and to cause further negative experiences leading to a downward spiralling of mood.

Beck described what he termed the cognitive triad. These are dysfunctional assumptions that lead to self-perpetuating and automatic negative cognitions. First, there is a negative self-view such as being worthless and unlovable; second, a negative view of the world as evidenced by past and present experiences. Finally, the future is viewed as being hopeless with the expectation that current problems will continue indefinitely.

The third component is the presence of cognitive errors. These are systematic logical errors in the thinking of depressed people. Beck has labelled different types of cognitive errors. The following are some examples.

- Magnification has occurred where events are evaluated as being more important than they are ('If I'm late they will think that I've decided to leave'.).
- Overgeneralisation is when one or more isolated incidents are exaggerated and applied to support a belief or rule ('This always happens to me. Everything always goes wrong.').
- Selective abstraction is where details are taken out of context and other details are ignored ('I got 75% for the test. How stupid of me to make so many mistakes.').
- Arbitrary inferences is where conclusions are made without supporting evidence ('My friend hasn't phoned me. She must have decided that she doesn't want to speak to me any more.').

Thoughts, feelings, behaviours and bodily reactions are continually inter-related in the present (Figure 2.2). A 'vicious circle' becomes established whereby the symptoms of depression become self-perpetuating.

A teenage girl has been experiencing problems at school, related to bullying and perceived criticism from her teachers (life situation). She feels very low and sad (mood) and has stopped going into school and going out with her friends, spending much of her time alone in her room

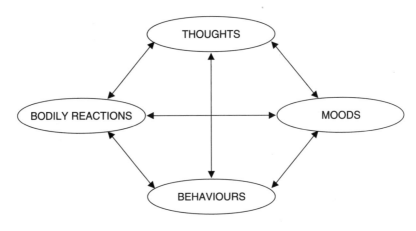

LIFE SITUATION

Figure 2.2   The cognitive hot cross bun (adapted from Padesky and Mooney, 1990)

(behaviour). In addition, she feels physically unwell and has frequent headaches (bodily reactions). Her main thoughts have been about being a failure and no one liking her.

Similar models of depression were developed at about the same time as that of Beck. Models with a greater emphasis on the behavioural aspects of depression followed the work of Martin Seligman on Learned Helplessness (Seligman, 1975). Lewinsohn and colleagues developed the Coping with Depression Course with adults focusing on the more behavioural elements of depression (Lewinsohn *et al.*, 1989). There has been extensive experimental research on cognitive models of depression in adults (see Clark and Fairburn, 1997).

> The cognitive behavioural model explores the relationship between thoughts, feelings and behaviour.
>
> Cognitive elements include schemata, negative automatic thoughts and cognitive errors.

Evidence for the cognitive model of depression in children and adolescents

In cognitive theory, depression is not simply triggered by adversity but rather by the perception and processing of adverse events. Research has shown that depressed young people have cognitive deficits and distortions, such as selectively attending to negative features of an event. In addition, depressed young people are more likely to have a negative attributional style. They tend to attribute the cause of positive events to unstable external causes rather than to their own endeavours. Depressed young people have also been shown to have low perceived academic and social competence.

Many studies have documented an association between childhood depression and cognitive distortions. It is unclear whether these negative cognitions are a cause or consequence of depression. For example, Dalgleish *et al.* (1998) reported that performance on information processing tasks returned to normal when depression remitted. It is also uncertain whether some cognitive processes are more important than others. Nevertheless, experimental research on cognitive processes has demonstrated the applicability of cognitive models to depression in young people.

CBT and stages of development in adolescence

Cognitive development is important in considering how the cognitive model for depression applies to children and for the practice of CBT. Children think differently from adults in some ways and consideration of this is important in appraising the applicability of a therapy derived from work on depressed adults.

The influential developmental psychologist Piaget divided intellectual development into four stages (Flavell, 1967). During the first stage of *sensori-motor thinking* the infant is not yet using language as a basis for thought. The second stage, the period of *pre-operational thought*, occurs between the ages of 18 months and 7 years. Thinking in this stage is limited, perceptions dominate cognition ('seeing is believing'). Children at this age tend to be focused on the present; thinking is often apparently illogical. This is the time of magical thinking, of nightmares and monsters.

Between the ages of 7 to 11 years there is the onset of Piaget's third stage, *concrete operational thought*. This period is characterised by conservation; the child learns to discover what is consistent in the course of any change. They begin to understand that things are not always what they seem. The child becomes more logical, communicative and less egocentric, a practical problem solver.

According to Piaget, formal thinking develops from around the age of 11 through to 16 years. Thinking skills are developed, so that the adolescent can develop hypotheses about the world, and start to reason and think in the abstract. They can think about thinking, and start to perceive the self much more in psychological than in physical terms.

There is variability between individuals in the timing of attainment of different cognitive stages but not the sequence. It cannot be assumed that children have the mental abilities to reflect on their own thinking, and hence to make use of some of the cognitive techniques used with adults. However, CBT is essentially a practical problem-solving therapy such that children using concrete operational thinking will be able to understand and manage most aspects of therapy.

It is important that assessment is made of the adolescent's developmental stage. Although a number of tests are available for assessing comprehension, and metacognition, their usefulness as a means of categorising adolescents for therapy is limited. With younger adolescents behavioural interventions, or simple step-wise techniques such as social problem-solving may be more successful. Life events and family contexts will also play a large part in determining the young person's ability to discuss emotional experiences.

> The young person's cognitive ability needs to be assessed informally and the cognitive demands of therapy modified accordingly.

Cognitive behaviour therapy

Beck's work with adults has been very influential in work with adolescents. Wilkes *et al.* (1994) and Stark (1990) devised manuals for treatment trials for individuals and groups respectively based on his programme. The more behavioural approach of Lewinsohn has been applied by Clarke and colleagues (2002, 2005) in a series of outcome trials for groups of depressed adolescents.

A major element of CBT consists of challenging negative styles of thinking and helping young people apppraise themselves, the world and the future more positively. Other techniques can help by focusing on problems that are commonly associated with mood disturbance, for instance problems with peer group relationships, anxiety symptoms and general life problems. Teaching young people techniques of problem-solving can help them to stand back from the problems they experience and think through an appropriate response. Young people can also be taught skills to improve their social relationships, particularly within their peer group. In addition, some symptoms of mood disturbance, for instance problems with sleep, poor concentration and feelings of anger can be targeted and helped specifically.

CBT in practice

Cognitive behaviour therapies work in the ***here and now***, even though the problems may date from events in the past. Therapy involves working on a one to one basis on goals and ***problems that are defined jointly*** with the young person. The clinician takes the role of a ***supportive educator*** who helps think around the problems and work out strategies during the sessions.

As 'educator' the clinician does not have the answers but works with the young person on the basis that they may have some ideas which are worth trying out. The young person is given the opportunity to try change. For instance, if the young person asks 'What do you want me to do?' the clinician would reply 'Well, what do you want to achieve here?' The clinician might go on to say 'Let's look and see what kinds of choices we have here for solving this problem.' It is important that the young person is supported in following through suggestions from the session into their everyday life.

CBT is designed to ***be flexible*** and to take into account the age, emotional literacy and cognitive maturity of the young person. All young people are helped to develop an emotional vocabulary and to identify problems and goals. With the younger, less reflective adolescent more concrete tasks will be used in contrast to the more mature group who are able to reflect on and work with their own thought processes.

It is important that parents, carers and professionals who have day to day contact with the young person are informed about how best they can support the work. This will vary with the individual case. However it is important to have regular meetings, which may also include the young person, to promote this.

> CBT is collaborative, tailored to the developmental level of the young person, with a here and now focus.

Working cognitively

CBT involves working with different aspects of thought and thinking. This can include:

- cognitive structures, for instance memories of childhood experiences
- content and information which may be used to appraise beliefs, such as about the nature of depression
- cognitive processes such as problem-solving. These are often distorted or ineffective in depressed young people
- cognitive products for instance beliefs and attributions, how we make sense of our context which may or may not be reality based.

Therapeutic methods and style of CBT

Many skills required for CBT are those required in any effective work with young people and their families and carers. A good knowledge of features of depression in adolescents and ability to assess suicidal wishes or ideas and behaviour through direct questions is essential. *Empathy* requires that the clinician experiences an accurate understanding of the young person's experience and is able to see the young person's personal world yet remain objective. It is important the young person perceives the clinician's empathy and acceptance. *Genuineness* involves the clinician reflecting accurately how they experience the young person's situation. *Warmth* is shown by empathy and positive unconditional regard for the young person.

Awareness of boundaries is very important in work with young people. The clinician is not a friend, circumstances in which confidentiality is maintained must be clear and the therapy requires a formal setting.

In general, therapy is delivered following referral to a specialist service. Following an initial assessment treatment options will be explored. Sometimes the therapy may be given by the child's key worker (for example, social worker, ward nurse). One advantage of this is that the key worker already has a relationship with the young person, so that some problems of engagement have already been overcome. However, as a therapist, the key worker is taking on a different role with the young person and the boundaries of this need to be clear. Ways of ensuring this are:

- giving the therapy a name
- clearly structuring the sessions i.e. having a set time, length of session, place and agenda, free from other distractions
- the therapy needs to be contained within the sessions. However, between sessions the key worker can use the opportunity for contact to gather information, model skills and remind the young person about tasks and home practice
- similarly, closure of therapy will need to be made clear. However, since the key worker will continue to have contact with the young person afterwards, there will be opportunities to continue to reinforce skills, and, if necessary, have 'booster' sessions.

CBT uses a ***collaborative approach*** and is ***goal orientated***. The collaborative relationship is established from the outset with jointly agreed goals and agendas. The young person needs to be prepared to practise techniques and record information in and out of the sessions.

The ***structure of CBT sessions*** is typically:

- review of young person's mood state and recent events
- set agenda
- review home practice
- work on session targets, for instance defining problems, identifying negative thoughts and challenging them
- establish home practice based on work during the session
- take feedback on the session and plan the next appointment.

CBT ***is time-limited*** and a likely number of sessions is usually agreed following assessment. The number of sessions typically ranges from 8 to 20. A session normally refers to approximately 45 minutes of individual work with the young person. It may be helpful to spend an additional 5 to 15 minutes with the parents being involved. The importance of parental participation will vary according to the age, background and specific problems that bring the young person to therapy. ***Home practice*** is an essential feature as it translates the techniques used in the sessions to home and allows generalisation of work in sessions. Recording home practice enables the clinician to gain valuable information for current and future sessions. CBT works with the adolescent in their social context, helping them to cope with everyday problems that they may be currently experiencing.

Overview of CBT techniques

CBT is model-driven and the approach taken will be determined by the individual formulation of a young person's difficulties. A range of techniques can be used as part of the process of tackling individual goals. These can involve cognitive and behavioural elements to different degrees.

Emotional recognition involves developing a shared vocabulary. The young person describes their understanding of difficult emotions. The therapist ensures that they understand how the young person expresses how they feel.

Activity scheduling involves the scheduling of enjoyable and goal-directed activities into the young person's day. This helps the young person combat the social withdrawal, passivity and apathy associated with an episode of depression. *Self-reward* encourages the use of rewards to promote positive behaviour and thinking. Depressed young people often have little sense of being rewarded. Low self-esteem inhibits them from rewarding themselves. In CBT young people learn to reward themselves after completing an activity, a coping strategy or home practice assignment.

Social skills training and *problem-solving skills training* can be helpful interventions. It is well established that depressive symptoms in young people are linked to impairment in social relationships with peers, parents and teachers (Harrington, 1999). Young people become socially withdrawn when depressed. Using role play and discussion the clinician can promote skill development.

Training in problem-solving can tackle the rigidity that can occur in the depressed person's thinking as it helps them to think logically and consider alternative solutions to situations. It also helps the young person overcome a sense of hopelessness as they see that there may be some options that they had not considered. In some cases, the young person becomes empowered as they experience success and a sense of mastery over the environment. For young people who are currently experiencing adverse situations, it can help them develop plans for overcoming, avoiding or lessening the impact.

Self-monitoring is used throughout therapy. The aim is to identify and monitor the presence of thoughts and feelings in different circumstances in everyday life using a diary. This assists the clinician in accessing negative automatic thoughts and core beliefs. *Cognitive restructuring* involves challenging negative automatic thoughts and beliefs and identifying thinking errors. The clinician can help the adolescent examine evidence and consider alternatives.

The conceptualisation of CBT involves the young person understanding that their thinking processes were distorted and that their negative automatic thoughts affect their feelings and behaviour. The clinician can help by sharing their *formulation* of how the core thoughts developed from that individual's past history. Thus the individual develops an understanding of the basis of their experience of depression. They have developed skills during the therapy that will enable them to deal with any future depressive feelings effectively.

Home practice is central to the process of therapy. Assignments are usually recorded in a diary or record sheets for the purpose. This reinforces the tasks covered in the sessions, and places them in the context of everyday life. It also provides valuable information for the clinician, including assessing the young person's motivation and psychological strengths.

Core components of CBT programmes for depression include:

- emotional recognition
- activity scheduling
- self-reward
- social skills training
- problem-solving
- self-monitoring
- cognitive restructuring.

A typical CBT programme for a depressed adolescent

Following referral for CBT, assessment first involves detailed clarification of symptoms, by interview and questionnaires, in order to establish a baseline for measuring change.

Goals for therapy are discussed, aiming to be as specific as possible. These are likely to include a goal to 'feel less depressed' but may include a range of associated problems identified by the child or young person. An explanation of the therapeutic process is given and the importance of home practice emphasised.

During the early sessions, work focuses on clarifying daily activities by discussion and diary keeping (activity scheduling). A check is made on the young person's vocabulary for describing feelings (emotional recognition) and links are made between activities and feelings. At this stage home practice tasks will be agreed that increase the range or number of activities from which the young person obtains a sense of achievement or pleasure. The emphasis is on re-instating previously enjoyed activities that have ceased and increasing normal day to day social routines rather than making special trips out. These behavioural interventions can often lead to a significant improvement in mood.

By this stage it is usually clear to what extent the young person is able to work at a cognitive level. For the less emotionally articulate the introduction of problem-solving techniques at this stage may be useful, for instance to work on peer group problems or issues at school.

A key aspect of cognitive therapy is that of identifying negative automatic thoughts. With young people, similarly to adults, this is approached by considering in detail the thoughts that occur in specific situations. In explaining this to young people the technique can be likened to video replay, playing back a situation and describing what you are thinking at the time. Diaries, creative writing or even statements from questionnaires can also be helpful in identifying maladaptive cognitions.

Processes of cognitive restructuring involve working on irrational interpretations and identifying recurrent themes such as being unlovable. This may include examining in detail the evidence for particular thoughts and the advantages and disadvantages of this way of thinking. In practice the techniques involve learning to recognise and challenge negative automatic thoughts, generating more realistic alternative thoughts and increasing positive statements about oneself. Once familiar with the approach, the experienced clinician can use a range of verbal and non-verbal methods and an understanding of children's social contexts and experience will assist in communicating effectively by using relevant examples and analogies. Therapeutic work with less articulate young people can focus on behavioural elements such as activity scheduling, self-reward and emotional recognition. Goals may include tackling associated problems such as study skills, assertiveness and problems with self-control.

In cognitive therapy with adults in recent years there has been a focus on addressing underlying cognitive schema. With children and adolescents this is rarely possible or indeed, necessary or appropriate. However, the young person will often develop an understanding of how their previous life experiences have contributed to the development of depression.

Closure of therapy includes a review of the previous themes of the therapy. The clinician stresses the links between the content of sessions and initial goals. The young person's active participation in the programme and their improvement in specific areas is acknowledged and reinforced.

The specific content and emphasis of the CBT programme will be informed by the assessment and formulation, therefore the actual content of individually constructed CBT will vary although a standard intervention might consist of the schema shown in Figure 2.3, accompanied by out of session assignments. The main focus of each session is highlighted although it is important to emphasise that each builds upon the previous sessions as the cognitive, behavioural and emotional components are integrated.

The evidence base for CBT for depressive disorders

Research trials

To date there have been about 50 randomised controlled trials (RCTs) evaluating psychological interventions for depression in young people. CBT is the basis of almost all of them and has been used in both school and clinical settings. There have been five meta-analyses with the most recent (Weisz *et al.*, 2006; Watanabe *et al.*, 2007) considering all psychological

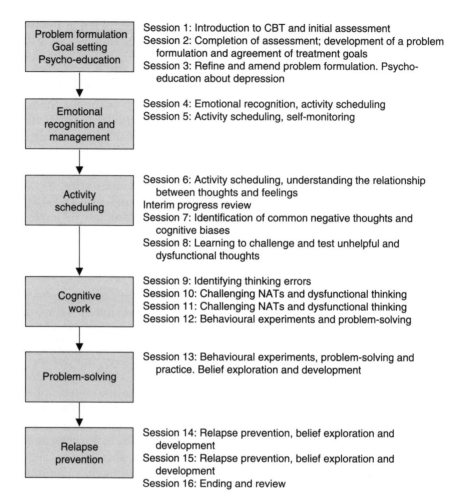

Figure 2.3   A standard cognitive behaviour therapy intervention

therapies. Of the earlier meta-analyses two were of CBT alone (Reinecke *et al.*, 1998; Lewinsohn and Clarke, 1999) and one of all psychological therapies (Michael and Crowley, 2002).

Weisz *et al.* (2006) reported a modest effect size for treatment compared with no treatment. In this analysis almost all studies were a form of CBT. Watanabe *et al.* (2007) similarly reported positive effects of psychotherapy, pooling data across many studies and commented that the largest body of evidence related to the effectiveness of CBT. Many RCTs have reported significant improvements in depression for young people with CBT. However, there are outstanding research design issues particularly in demonstrating that treatment gains persist over time. Fonagy *et al.* (2002) draw attention to the greater effectiveness of CBT in studies using specially recruited as opposed to clinically referred children.

Clinical guidance

The National Institute for Health and Clinical Excellence (NICE, 2005a) clinical guideline on depression in children and young people identified 18 trials of psychological treatment published between 1986 and 2004 that met eligibility criteria. There were 14 from the USA, 3 from Europe and 1 from Puerto Rico. The majority involved an element of CBT. Four involved individual CBT with clinic populations and seven involved group CBT. The guideline concluded that for individual outcomes, the quality of the research evidence was generally moderate to low, relecting the paucity of data and relatively small sample sizes of the studies. The overall evidence of the effectiveness of CBT was judged inconclusive; two studies showed similar outcomes to wait list or general management and three a superior outcome for CBT. At 6 months differences between groups were no longer apparent due to improvement in the untreated groups. Considerable evidence of the effectiveness of group CBT was identified on recruited samples in the USA. All treatments tend to show less effect over time compared with the control interventions. Untreated groups improve over time. No adequately designed relapse prevention studies were identified.

Because of the diverse nature of the studies, clinician and patient characteristics that contribute to outcome are not consistently identified. However, the following are generally associated with poorer outcomes: severity, co-morbidity, chronicity, suicidality and high levels of hopelessness, higher levels of cognitive distortion. Poor parenting and higher family dysfunction were also predictive of negative outcome (Emslie *et al.*, 2003; Brent *et al.*, 1997). The presence of child abuse and trauma was widely shown to be correlated with higher rates of depression and more difficulty in treatment (Meyerson *et al.*, 2002). The NICE report concludes that there is evidence that professionally trained clinicians have better results and that a positive treatment alliance predicts better outcome.

CBT in groups

A group CBT programme, the 'Adolescent Coping with Depression Course' (Clarke *et al.*, 1990) has been successfully evaluated in a number of studies in the USA (see Clarke *et al.*, 2002). Groups have been of six to ten young people and are usually based in schools. The group format consists of sixteen 2-hour sessions, often with up to three booster sessions to maintain treatment gains. The group leaders teach CBT skills including relaxation techniques, cognitive restructuring, increasing the frequency of pleasant activities and communication and conflict reduction techniques. The primary theoretical model is of social learning and the groups are based on the work of Lewinsohn with adults. The sessions involve role play and there is a workbook for all participants for homework exercises. There are three parallel sessions for parents providing information about the general topics discussed, skills taught and rationale for their use.

> RCTs and meta-analysis demonstrate that CBT results in significant post-treatment gains. There is less evidence to demonstrate that these gains are maintained over time.

3

Cognitive behavioural assessment and formulation

It is important to note that many depressed young people will present to agencies with problems other than mood having been identified. Young people often do not take the initiative themselves in seeking help. Help may be sought on their behalf by parents, carers or teachers who have noticed behavioural changes such as irritability or problems in relationships. Assessment may have several purposes. In the first interview the major goal is usually to identify how the agency or resource can best help the young person. This may first involve a diagnosis of the presenting problems and discussing options for intervention. This may be the first time that the young person's depressive symptoms are noted. A further assessment may be undertaken to develop a cognitive behavioural problem formulation and to establish goals and baselines for change. It can be helpful to the engagement process if the same practitioner is involved at all stages.

Principles of assessment

Assessment and intervention are to some extent parallel processes. The development of a working relationship and collaborative approach begins at the first contact. In everyday practice the clinician or their colleagues immediately begin shaping the young person and their parents' approach to the problems that prompted the consultation. Considerations such as who is present at the interview, the focus of questions and interviewer responses to answers may influence family members' expectations and attitudes. The process of interview is likely to influence changes in the young person and parents' perspectives from the outset for instance about responsibility for the problem, the potential for change and appreciation of the nature or severity of difficulties.

Intervention begins with assessment; assessment also continues throughout treatment. This may involve continuing assessment of key problem areas, to monitor change, or opening a fresh area of assessment as a result of identification of a new problem or moving to a new stage of therapy. For instance, after the first few individual sessions a young person may reveal previously undisclosed concerns about academic performance. These concerns may warrant further assessment including, for instance, contacting teachers or assessment of intellectual ability and educational attainment. Moving on to another stage in therapy may involve assessing new areas, for instance activity scheduling includes assessing routine activities. School attendance may then be established as a problem.

Assessment involves obtaining information from a range of sources and is likely to involve several methods. Many aspects of behaviour and performance are dependent on features of the setting in which they occur and a fuller appreciation of problems may be gained by seeking information as widely as is practical. The clinician uses both subjective and objective methods. Routine assessments should include baseline measures of progress that may include behaviour rating scales, task performance measures, self-report measures and, less commonly, behavioural observation.

An essential aspect of assessment is the clinician's observation of important factors in therapy such as the young person's ability to form a working rapport with the interviewer, their verbal abilities and evidence of the commitment of parents to supporting therapy.

> Depressive symptoms may not be the reason for seeking help.
>
> Assessment will need to consider all areas of the young person's life.
>
> Regular assessment and monitoring are important features of cognitive behaviour therapy (CBT).

Problem-focused assessment

A problem-focused approach can be helpful in identifying a young person's suitability for cognitive behaviour therapy. In many settings clinicians obtain detailed information as a routine aspect of the service using a combination of parent, individual and family interviews. Interviewing the young person individually at some stage during the assessment is essential. The information below is generally obtained. This will contribute to the broader understanding of the development of the young person's strengths and difficulties and may be used as the basis for diagnostic or aetiological formulation.

Areas for assessment

- Problem details and route to referral; what is the problem and why is help being sought now?
- Significant life events including recent and remote changes of likely relevance.
- Developmental history and medical problems.
- Educational history and attainment.
- Temperament and social relationships.
- Family history and circumstances.
- Parent–child relationship.
- Family relationship problems for instance marital discord.
- Family stressors for instance housing, neighbours.
- Previous treatment and outcome.

Cultural context

The clinician must be mindful of the cultural context of the young person's problems. It may be that they regularly experience racism, social deprivation or feel undervalued by society due to their culture, ethnicity, religion or sexual orientation.

Cultural awareness is likely to be a general part of the clinician's practice. This should include listening carefully to understand the importance of a client's culture and to consider ways in which a client's culture influences conceptualisation and treatment planning. The clinician may need to educate themselves about different cultures including consulting with colleagues who have relevant cultural expertise. It is also important to discuss with young people their experiences within their community and seek feedback on the cultural assumptions of therapy and its procedures.

Confidentiality

Issues of confidentiality will also need to be addressed so that the young person and their carers are clear from the outset as to what information may be shared. The clinician will need to be honest about the limits of confidentiality with the young person, explaining that their sessions will be private but that if the clinician has concerns about the young person's safety then this will need to be discussed with other people particularly parents or carers. Also that information which is to be shared will generally be discussed first with the young person. Parents and carers may need to understand that only in these circumstances will information be shared and that they will not be told details of specifics of assessment sessions as reported by the young person to the clinician. General issues in the assessment of suicidality are considered in Chapter 10.

Interviews with parents or carers

Clinicians differ in how they approach obtaining information from parents and carers. From a collaborative perspective, it is important to include the young person in the interview. Interviewing parents together with the young person provides useful observational information on family relationships and differing perspectives on problems. There may be some information personal to parents that requires them to be seen on their own. Typically this relates to parents' own psychological problems, marital problems or other situations of family conflict.

Parents provide very important information about the young person's functioning both generally and in relation to problem areas. It is important that they are invited to contribute in relation to strengths as well as difficulties. They should be asked to define problem behaviours. Often people give general statements in response and the interviewer may need to ask for specific examples, including antecedents and consequences of the behaviour. The parents may have tried to address problems and any attempts can be discussed. Details will need to be obtained of the course of the problem and any changes in frequency or intensity.

> *Tracey's parents complained about her stealing from them and lying about her activities. The clinician clarified details of when this had occurred and their response. Two incidents were described when small sums of money had been taken when Tracey had been forbidden from leaving the house. On her return she had denied stealing and refused to talk about where she had been. In response her parents had stopped her pocket money and forbidden her from going out after school for a month.*

Parents can reflect on longer term changes over the young person's lifetime.

> *Tracey's parents reported that Tracey had a slow start in social relationships when starting school and seemed quite isolated. She then successfully made friends in the later stages of primary school. When she started at High school she seemed to be on her own quite a lot of the time and her parents had wondered if she was trying to 'buy friendship'.*

It is important not to rely exclusively on parents' views particularly when assessing the mood and personal feelings of the young person. There is research evidence that adults, including parents, consistently under-report negative mood symptoms in young people (Angold *et al.*, 1998b).

It is also important for the clinician to gain an impression of how parents establish their expectations of their children, their approach to child rearing and about firmly held views about family life. This provides a helpful context in discussions with the young person in sessions when the clinician may need to help generate practical ideas.

Helpful information from parents and carers includes:

- definition of problems
- the young person's strengths
- parent–child relationships
- family stressors including marital difficulties.

Individual assessment: the first interview

Adolescents will have a different perspective on problems from their parents. They may not feel comfortable talking in the presence of their parents and some information, particularly regarding their feelings and suicidal thoughts should be sought during an individual interview. Where there is conflict between family members, it is important that the clinician explains that they are not judging right or wrong but are interested in understanding the different points of view.

Tracey's mother reported that her daughter has been seen out with a small group of her friends, laughing together in a relaxed manner. Tracey described a sense of failure in her social life and feels that she has to struggle to keep in the group. Both views are accurate. Their implications are different. Tracey felt that she did not wish to burden her mother with her social anxiety.

A mental state assessment of the young person will need to take place at an early stage. It is important to identify key symptoms of depressive disorder including level of mood, excessive guilt, suicidal ideation and behaviour and presence of any psychotic symptoms such as delusions and hallucinations.

Symptoms of depression/criteria for major depressive episode (DSM-IV)

At least five present for 2 weeks must include one of *:

- *depressed mood most of the day, nearly everyday

- irritability, temper outbursts
- *demonstrated loss of interest or pleasure in activities
- weight loss when not dieting or weight gain due to loss of appetite or comfort eating
- insomnia or hypersomnia
- agitation or retardation
- fatigue, loss of energy
- feelings of worthlessness, guilt
- diminished ability to think or concentrate, indecisiveness
- recurrent thoughts of death, fear of dying, suicidal ideation, suicide attempt, plan of suicide.

Symptoms cause distress. Impairment in functioning that is not caused by physical illness or acute life event. Persistence of symptoms for more than 2 months may be considered abnormal.

Symptoms of depression such as social withdrawal and loss of concentration can make depressed individuals very difficult to assess. For example, they may have difficulty responding to open questions that invite descriptive answers. It may, on occasions, be necessary to be more direct, e.g., by providing examples of the type of symptoms they might be experiencing.

Particular care needs to be taken to establish a vocabulary that the young person uses to describe how they feel. Similarly, clarifying duration and fluctuations in these feelings can require skill. Again, using concrete examples can be helpful. Linking feelings to specific situations and identifying particularly distressing thoughts begins the process of applying a cognitive behavioural framework.

Another key task of the first individual interview is to assess the young person's interest and motivation for individual work. It is often not the young person themselves who has been instrumental in seeking help. They may have resisted attending. Pacing of the interviews is necessary in order to allow for a shift in the young person's attitude as the nature of the assessment becomes clearer to them. Reassurance about help seeking and understanding ambivalence may be required. The young person's understanding of their difficulties and the purposes of referral must be explored. Problem examples or difficult episodes can be tracked. On other occasions the clinician may find it helpful to use hypothetical examples of similar problems and another young person's view to provoke discussion. In the course of discussion levels of distress that the problem causes will be clarified and also attitudes to difficulties, motivation for change and attributions about the source of difficulties.

The clinician begins asking about thoughts and feelings in relation to specific situations and problem areas at this stage.

An individual interview with the young person is essential to establish the nature of depressive symptoms and diagnostic features. In addition this will involve beginning to use cognitive behavioural frameworks in detailed definition of problems and related thoughts and feelings.

Assessing suitability for individual CBT

Type of problem

Cognitive behavioural approaches are suitable for young people with mood disturbances, particularly depression or anxiety. Depressive symptoms may be a feature of a wider problem and may not have been identified by the young person or their parent as the main problem. A current problem involving cognitive distortions such as a negative self-appraisal or cognitive behavioural deficits such as problems with social skills is a pre-requisite for CBT. It is important to emphasise that, although behavioural difficulties do not of themselves exclude young people from CBT, young people who have long standing or severe acting out behaviours, such as absconding or stealing, may be harder to engage in CBT. Similarly, young people who are very preoccupied with other issues in their lives, such as their home situation or thoughts about past experiences are also less likely to be helped. For this reason, young people who are currently involved in legal or criminal proceedings will sometimes be unsuitable. A tendency to externalise or attribute reasons for difficulties solely to other people or external situations is an important factor which is generally predictive of poor engagement.

> *John presented to the service as a bright 13-year-old with a 6-month history of school absences, which began when the family moved to the area. Due to the nature of family relationship difficulties the main focus of work was planned to be family therapy and liaison with teachers about John's school situation. John himself was depressed and talked about the impact of losses of his friends. He felt that he was no longer able to make friends and wanted help with this, so individual CBT was agreed alongside family sessions.*

Characteristics of the individual young person

For a young person to be able to take on individual CBT the following factors need to be considered by the clinician.

- The young person must be able to identify a suitable focus for work.
- It is important that the young person perceives potential for control of the problem, at least in part.

- The individual must also be able to take some responsibility for change for instance by agreeing to try out different ways of tackling a situation.
- The young person needs to be able to discuss situations from their own and other people's perspectives and be able to describe how they feel.

The therapeutic approach of CBT is predominantly verbal and may be less suitable, or requires modification, for young people who have difficulty in expressing themselves. The approach has been used successfully with children and adolescents within the normal range of intellectual ability. Emotional literacy is probably more important than intellectual ability.

> *Andrew had been suspended from school following an incident of aggression with his peers. He had received several warnings in situations where he had lost his temper. He and his parent sought the assistance of a clinician in preparing his return to school. His parents reported that they had no concerns about Andrew's behaviour at home. Andrew was distressed by his situation but expressed the view that he had been treated unjustly. He wanted to return to school. The clinician undertook two individual assessment sessions. During these it did not prove possible to identify behaviours that Andrew wanted to change nor attitudes that were open to challenge. The clinician decided that individual cognitive behaviour therapy was not a suitable approach.*

Characteristics of the context

Therapy with individual children and adolescents requires support from parents or carers in several respects.

- There must be assistance in the practical aspects of attendance and a genuine interest in progress.
- The home environment should be supportive, at least in organisational terms, for completion of home practice tasks.
- It is important to consider whether the time is optimal. If the current situation is unstable or about to change, for instance if a young person in local authority care is about to change foster placement then a more generally supportive intervention may be required in the first instance. In some circumstances individual CBT may be identified as appropriate once a particular crisis has been overcome or once a family situation has stabilised.
- Where a parent–child relationship is conflicted, negative or ambivalent it is important that appropriate work is also undertaken with the parents or family together.

Parents and carers will continue some involvement with individual CBT following assessment. This is discussed in Chapter 9.

> *Gemma's parents separated three years before referral and Gemma had maintained a good relationship with her father who lived nearby with his*

new family. Gemma and her mother had both experienced depression since the death of Gemma's grandfather a year earlier. Her mother planned to move house to be able to provide more support to her own mother but Gemma wished to stay. Gemma's father offered her a home. The clinician decided that the current uncertainty was a significant factor in Gemma's mood disturbance and work primarily with her parents was undertaken before individual CBT was started.

Suitability for individual CBT

Type of problem:

- identified by young person
- definable
- evidence of cognitive or behavioural distortion/deficit
- consensus view obtained from parents/carers
- amenable to change.

Individual:

- can be engaged in individual approach/agrees to attend
- can take responsibility
- moderate depression i.e. not overwhelming levels of depressive-ness nor psychotic symptoms
- risk assessment and risk management plan in place
- no significant learning/communication difficulties
- evidence of empathy, abilities to understand and consider others' thoughts/views.

Context:

- practical support from parents/carers in attending sessions
- consensus from parents/carers on need/appropriateness of individual approach
- agreement of parents/carers to be involved in therapy
- environment safe and some stability evident
- other agencies involved in treatment agree, coordination evident.

Use of standardised interviews

The National Institute for Health and Clinical Excellence (NICE) Guideline on Depression in Children and Young People (2005a) drew attention to the use of standardised interview schedules in identification of depressive symptoms. Several are available for use with children and adolescents. Their primary purpose has been to provide diagnoses for research purposes. All include a wide range of diagnoses, are reported to be reliable in the assessment of depression, and will identify co-morbid conditions, for instance anxiety or conduct disorder. Training in administration is required to ensure that diagnoses are made reliably. They can also be used by clinicians who wish to evaluate a wide range of symptoms in a standardised fashion. In these circumstances the choice of interview will depend on the skills of the interviewer and whether or not assessment of change is a consideration. All of the interviews are suitable for adolescents but vary as to their lower age limit.

The Schedule for Affective Disorders and Schizophrenia for School-Age Children (K-SADS; Puig-Antich and Ryan, 1978: Kaufman *et al.*, 1997) is a semi-structured interview for 6–17-year-olds and is widely used in research studies of affective disorders in young people. It is designed to be administered by experienced clinicians and is organised according to diagnostic categories. The severity of depression is assessed. NICE (2005a) recommended this as an instrument for improving the accuracy of child mental health professionals in detecting depressive conditions. It is lengthy to administer for routine clinical use.

The Diagnostic Interview for Children and Adolescents (DICA; Reich, 2000) and Diagnostic Interview Schedule for Children (DISC; Costello *et al.*, 1985) are both designed to be administered by trained lay interviewers and require a minimum of clinical inference. The Child and Adolescent Psychiatric Assessment (CAPA; Angold and Costello, 2000) incorporates interview and questionnaire approaches and can be used with 9–16-year-olds. The Development and Well-Being Assessment (DAWBA; Meltzer *et al.*, 2000) is a package of questionnaires, interviews and rating scales for psychiatric diagnosis in 5–16-year-olds.

Diagnostic interview measures are, in general, less useful measures of change than questionnaire measures. This is because they are designed to measure presence or absence of a diagnosis rather than identify gradual changes. The severity ratings incorporated in the measures are useful. The interviews are lengthy and time consuming for routine repeated use.

General level of psychological adjustment

There are several general behaviour questionnaire and rating scales available that the young person's parent, carer or teacher completes and which provide norms according to age and gender. These have the advantage of being quick and easy to complete and score. Most of them sample a range of the child's or adolescent's behaviour and so may provide a more general information base. More detailed clinical assessment of depressive symptoms will always be required in addition.

Strengths and Difficulties Questionnaires (Goodman, 1997; www. sdqinfo.com). These are questionnaires for children, adolescents, parents and teachers that cover a wide range of problems including emotional, behavioural and social difficulties and are often used as baseline and follow-up measures or as part of routine assessment procedures.

Child Behaviour Checklist (Achenbach, 1991). There are parent and teacher versions which are used for children aged 4–16 years. The checklist has 118 items each with 0, 1, 2 scoring and 3 additional social competency scales. There are norms for 4–5, 6–11, 12–16 year groups. These checklists are used extensively for clinical and research purposes.

Assessment of specific areas of functioning

Assessment of intellectual ability and educational attainment

The best assessment of whether or not a child has the cognitive capacity to cope with a verbal reflective therapy is the problem-focused interview. Intellectual ability is not a reliable discriminator in this respect. However, it may be important to assess intellectual ability for other purposes for instance examining possible reasons for school failure. Some people with unusual cognitive profiles have a high level of verbal fluency which conceals significant difficulties in other areas. When this is suspected clarification through psychometric testing may be helpful.

Task performance measures

Many tasks can be used to obtain observational data on metacognition (the ability to reflect on one's own thought processes), strategies for problem-solving, handling frustration, self-awareness and response to praise.

Social problem-solving

These are often particularly useful in individual or group interventions as a basis for discussion. Cartoons that demonstrate social situations can be used to assess social cognition. In these, young people look at a cartoon situation and are asked to describe what is going on. Interpersonal dilemmas can be used to identify concepts of friendship and peer group relationship skills. They involve descriptions of situations involving conflict of interest that invite the child to identify and explain the course of action they would suggest. Problem-solving tasks present scenarios that are designed to identify ability to take a systematic approach to solving a problem. Clinicians are often involved in designing their own examples that are relevant to the young person's daily context.

> *Ahmed age 13 had been referred because of his low mood. Although he had a history of being bullied in primary school, he had recently been*

involved in initiating severe bullying incidents in school. Assessment included discussion of some scenarios of bullying from the perspective of victim and instigator in order to clarify Ahmed's attitudes and beliefs.

Self-efficacy

Measures that identify the young person's ability to manage or control aspects of their environment and how positive they feel about their attempts can be particularly important in working with therapeutic techniques which tackle negativity.

Eliciting causal attributions is frequently part of the process of enquiry during interviews. It is important to recognise how the form of a question can influence responses. Children's Attributional Style Questionnaire (CASQ-R) (Thompson *et al.*, 1998) is designed for 8–13-year-olds to assess how children attribute causality to good and bad events. Spontaneous attributions of causality are particularly valuable and are used as clinical material in cognitive restructuring.

There are several self-report questionnaires available of self-concept/ self-esteem. The Piers–Harris (Piers *et al.*, 2002), Self-Perception Profile for Children (Harter, 1985) and Self Esteem Inventory (Coopersmith 1967, 1975) are all in widespread use.

Mood

Self-report measures are very useful as many are designed both for assessment in relation to norms and as measures of change. Many clinicians use specific measures as a matter of routine on a regular basis throughout therapy. They are also useful as indicators of severity of depressive symptoms. Most mood checklists were developed for use with adults and then modified and re-standardised for use with younger age groups. It is often worth considering using the adult versions with older adolescents as norms for adults frequently go down to age 16 years and the adult versions often have more extensive norms and better established reliability and validity. The questionnaires generally give a series of questions asking young people to record how they have been feeling and thinking over a recent time period (usually 1 or 2 weeks). The functional literacy of the young person will need to be considered before using such instruments.

Depression

The Children's Depression Inventory (27 items, age 7–12 years: Kovaacs, 1982), Beck Depression Inventory for Youth (20 item, age 7–14 years: Beck *et al.*, 2005) and Beck Depression Inventory (II) (Beck *et al.*, 1996) are all based on the original Beck Depression Inventory (Beck *et al.*, 1961) for adults.

The Depression Self-Rating Scale (age 9–13 years; Birleson *et al.*, 1987) and Mood and Feelings Questionnaires (MFQ 8–17 years: Costello and

Angold, 1988) are regularly used in clinical practice. The MFQ has long (33 item), short (13 item) and parent versions. These are all statistically reliable and valid measures for assessment and of change.

Anxiety

The Revised Children's Manifest Anxiety Scales (RCMAS: Reynolds and Richmond, 1985) and Spielberger State Trait Anxiety Inventory – Children's version (age 9–12 years; STAI-C: Spielberger *et al.*, 1983) can be very useful when the young person experiences anxiety as well as depression. These are measures for assessment and measuring change.

Post traumatic stress disorder

Several measures have been designed for assessment of symptoms of post traumatic stress disorder (PTSD). The nature of PTSD and its relevance to depression is considered in Chapter 10. The Impact of Event Scale (Horowitz *et al.*, 1979) was designed for adult populations but has also been used with children. Where trauma has included sexual abuse specific measures such as the Sexual Abuse Fear Evaluation (Wolfe and Wolfe, 1986) can be used to assess fears relating to events and situations that sexually abused children report as distressing. This is a 17-item scale embedded within the Fear Survey Schedule for Children – Revised (Ollendick, 1983). The Children's Impact of Traumatic Events (Wolfe *et al.*, 1991) has also been reported as useful in the assessment of sexual abuse.

Measures specific to CBT

Beck's cognitive theory identifies several levels of cognition. Self-report questionnaires have been developed for recognition of schema, dysfunctional attitudes and negative automatic thoughts in adults. Some adult versions of questionnaires have been tried with adolescent populations and some modified specifically for a younger age group.

The following are available for young people:

- Schema questionnaire (short form) (Young, 1998, revised for adolescents by Simmons *et al.*, 2006)
- Schema questionnaire for Children (Stallard and Rayner, 2005)
- Automatic Thoughts Questionnaire (ATQ) child version (Stark *et al.*, 1990) indicates the number of automatic thoughts that children are experiencing
- Cognitive Triad Inventory for Children (CTI-C) is a 36-item scale comprising three subscales: view of self, view of world and view of future (Kaslow *et al.*, 1992)
- Hopelessness Scale for Children (HSC; Kazdin *et al.*, 1983) is a 17-item self-report measure based on the measure for adults.

Recording and self-monitoring

As recording and self-monitoring play a key therapeutic role in cognitive behavioural treatments it can be very useful to start this as part of the assessment process. This provides an early assessment of difficulties in the completion of home practice tasks as well as obtaining baseline data and further information about problems. This can be set up with the young person and may involve parents. A diary, charts or a personalised checklist can be used.

The conclusion of formal assessment

The conclusion of formal assessment can be defined as the point when the clinician has a working rapport with the young person and parent, information from a range of sources has been obtained, depression diagnosis identified, specific problems and difficulties established, any complementary strengths identified and a consensus on goals of intervention achieved. A monitoring system for progress with parents when appropriate will be in place and work begun on a problem formulation in cognitive behavioural terms.

> Formal interview schedules can be useful in identifying symptoms of depression.
>
> There is a wide range of questionnaire measures which help clarify specific problem areas, broaden assessment information and allow measurement of progress in therapy.

Psycho-education

The diagnosis of depression is often very helpful in assisting the young person and their parents understand the nature of the presenting difficulties. In particular it may help by framing the difficult, challenging behaviour of some adolescents in non-judgemental terms. The understanding of irritability rather than sadness as a primary feature of depression in adolescence can be specifically mentioned. Reference to any family history of depression may help de-mystify and set the stage for parental involvement. Explanation of the nature of depression can help distance the young person from the symptoms in a helpful way. The adolescent is in a sense a victim of the depression that all can assist in beating with appropriate treatment. General information about the nature of depression can be provided before moving on to conceptualise the young person's experience on a more individual basis from a cognitive behavioural perspective. An information sheet can be provided (see Materials and worksheets).

Cognitive behavioural formulation

Over the course of the assessment, and the starting phase of CBT, the clinician has an opportunity to gain an understanding of the young person's presentation: the meaning and function of their symptoms, why they are presenting with problems at the current time, the precipitating and maintaining factors and the young person's strengths, weaknesses and supports. It is helpful at this point to draw this together into a cognitive behavioural formulation, referred to a case conceptualisation by some authors (Friedberg and McClure, 2002). This can be used with the young person in therapy and will be modified during the course of the intervention. Developing a cognitive behavioural formulation is similar to developing an aetiological or diagnostic formulation. The presenting symptoms are formulated as occurring in the setting of emotional reactions and cognitive deficits and distortions that have developed over time in response to early experiences. It is helpful for the clinician to speculate as to the underlying beliefs, assumptions and thinking errors and to the roots of these in terms of the young person's life experiences. Some elements may not be evident early in therapy. Formulation hypotheses can be tested later in therapy. The processes of the early stages of therapy are represented in Figure 3.1.

It is important that the young person understands the theoretical model of CBT and depression. The cognitive model suggests that their difficulties have arisen from cognitive distortions and skill deficits.

Early on in therapy the clinician will share a formulation with the young

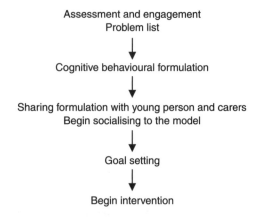

Figure 3.1   Early stages of cognitive behaviour therapy

person involving them as actively as possible. Increasing awareness that, for instance, their problems can be understood and that others experience similar feelings can have a positive benefit. A conceptualisation of difficulties can reduce distress and promote a hopeful approach. Each individual needs to have the cognitive model of depression personalised for them so that they can see where their own thoughts, feelings and behaviour and life events fit with the model. This creates a map of their own life experience and will help to explain how they have developed problems and symptoms. Also it helps to review what strategies have been tried and why they help or do not help. It also provides a rationale for the various treatment interventions that will be tried and helps to further engage young people in collaborating with the clinician.

The formulation will also generate hypotheses about what is maintaining the depression as well as potentially revealing core beliefs. The clinician will be returning to the formulation regularly throughout therapy in order to assess their hypothesis and to guide the intervention.

Sharing a formulation in practice

When sharing a formulation it is important that it is simple and straight forward and that both the young person and clinician feel that it fits well with information available. It will pinpoint questions that need answering so that both the clinician and young person understand better what is maintaining the problems and how they can be addressed.

The clinician may begin with a diagram representing the model (see Figure 3.2).

The clinician starts by taking the presenting problem and breaking it down into the components of the 'hot cross bun' i.e. mood, thoughts,

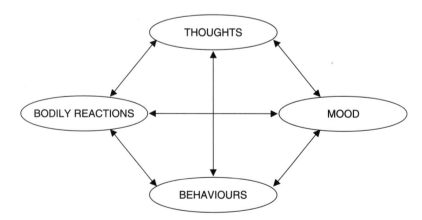

Figure 3.2　The cognitive behavioural hot cross bun (adapted from Padesky and Mooney, 1990)

behaviour and bodily reactions. Thus a personalised psychological picture starts to be developed.

The clinician uses the information gathered to begin to make links to the model. This is done collaboratively with the young person and helps to clarify their experiences, behaviour patterns, biological reactions, mood and thoughts. These are ultimately set in the context of their culture, development, environment and intrapersonal and interpersonal relationships. A first stage formulation may involve simply making links in the here and now between thoughts, feelings and behaviour around a particular difficulty.

> *John, age 12, has become low in mood and is withdrawn. The school raised concerns with his mother who went to see their family doctor, resulting in a referral to child and adolescent mental health services (CAMHS). The assessment confirmed a diagnosis of depression. This was in the context of John's parents separating 6 months earlier. Since then contact has been infrequent with his father. John was very close to his father and spent considerable time with him. John is the eldest of three children and it comes to light that his mother suffers from depression. John has felt increasingly concerned about his mother since his father left. This has reached a level where he does not want to leave her to go to school and he feels she needs him to care for her.*

When the clinician talks about these problems and the effect on him he is able to share the following (see Figure 3.3):

- he feels sad and tearful and gets anxious when is mum is unwell (feelings)
- he has lost interest in football and playing with his friends. Also that he tries to avoid going to school to stay at home with his mother (behaviour)

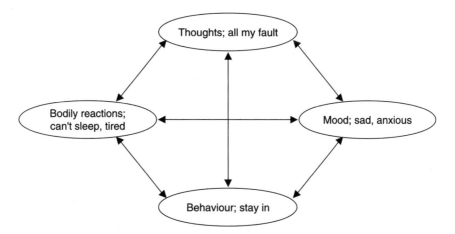

Figure 3.3 John's problem formulation; what happens when his mother is unwell

- he feels like he has no energy, lost his appetite and finds it hard to get to sleep (bodily reactions)
- he feels that it is all his fault and that things will never get any better (thoughts).

The critical incident that triggered John's depression was his father leaving home. This made his mother become more depressed. Both of these factors affected John.

The following is a detailed case example with a more comprehensive cognitive behavioural formulation that helps demonstrate the development of problems as well as how Emma's depression has been maintained.

Emma, aged 15 years, was referred by her family doctor with symptoms of depression and long-term problems with school attendance with complete school refusal for the month prior to assessment. Emma's mother had persuaded Emma to come for the initial appointment and said that she had completely given up trying to get Emma to go to school and had become very concerned about Emma's moodiness and lack of friends. Emma lived with her four older sisters and mother who worked full time as an administrator for a voluntary organisation. Emma's parents separated when she was 8 years of age and her father was now re-married with a 5-year-old daughter. Emma's mother acknowledged that she had found it difficult to bring up the five girls after her husband had left and had suffered from depression and anxiety since. She frequently had time off work and suffers from multiple somatic symptoms and presents as having chronic dysphoria. She had received support from her family doctor but had never had any psychiatric treatment for depression. An older sister also had a history of poor school attendance. She missed her final year at secondary school and was currently attending a sixth form college. Emma's oldest sisters both had boyfriends and were in work. There was no other family history of psychiatric disorder. Emma herself had no past medical history of relevance and her developmental and early educational history were uneventful until the age of 9 years when she became reluctant to attend primary school. At this time, her mother changed her school however the problems continued. Emma was bright academically but had always been shy and found it difficult to make and sustain peer relationships. Since starting at a large mainstream mixed secondary school, Emma's attendance had been sporadic. She achieved well in the first and second years but had found the last 2 years increasingly difficult.

At interview, Emma described feeling depressed 'for years' but much worse for the last 3–4 months. She was unable to relate her moods to any life event however acknowledged that they started in relation to school. She described extremely low moods with associated thoughts of hopelessness and self-harm. Emma admitted to cutting her wrists superficially on a number of occasions and also to taking small overdoses of paracetamol that she had not told anyone about. She thought that there was no possibility of anyone or anything helping her. Emma, in her appear-ance, looked older than her years. A tall girl with dyed blond hair tied in numerous plaits and beaded, she was wearing fairly heavy makeup and dressed in black with heavy boots. She had piercings in both ears and also a nose stud.

For the first interview, Emma answered questions with monosyl-lables and became tearful when telling of the longstanding nature of her problems. She was reluctant to speak at all in front of her mother and said that 'She has never understood me'. As well as depressed moods, Emma described poor concentration, lack of pleasure in anything, poor sleep, low self-esteem, a lack of self-confidence and overconcern about her weight and body image. She described a chaotic eating pattern with periods of dieting and some binge eating. She denied self-induced vomiting or laxative abuse and presented as of average weight for her height. Despite her eating habits, her weight did not fluctuate very much although she thought that she had gained weight over the last 3 months as a result of being at home so much of the time.

Cognitive behavioural formulation for Emma

Having completed a detailed assessment of Emma's presenting problems, the clinician drew together the strands of the assessment by representing the cognitive formulation diagrammatically (see Figure 3.4). Following the first or second appointments, it may be possible to do this provisionally, with many aspects often becoming clearer over time. Details of thoughts and beliefs often do not emerge until later in therapy. The purpose of formulat-ing the case is to facilitate treatment planning and cognitive working. The formulation is an evolving understanding of the young person, their pre-dicament and their current problems within their family and school context. The symptoms are delineated followed by a description of negative automatic thoughts, assumptions and cognitive style. How these faulty mechanisms developed and came to influence mood and behaviour are discussed. This is followed by a summary of aetiological factors and a comment about the young person's strengths and weaknesses in being able to benefit from CBT.

- Emma presents with the following difficulties:
  - **affective:** depressed moods, anger, anxiety
  - **motivational:** loss of interest and pleasure, everything too much effort
  - **behavioural:** avoidance of school and social situations, inactivity
  - **cognitive:** hopelessness, suicidal thoughts, self-blame, low self-esteem, poor concentration, overconcern with appearance/body weight
  - **somatic:** loss of sleep, tiredness, disturbed eating patterns.
- Early experience: Emma is the youngest and was aged 8 years when her father left. She always compared herself unfavourably with her older sisters and felt that her father never had any time for her. For most of

her early years her parents' marriage was under stress and when her father left, Emma felt pleased. During these years her mother was intermittently depressed. Emma felt unwanted by both of her parents.

- Core beliefs: I'm worthless. I am inferior as a person. I am unlovable.
- Assumptions: If people get to know the real me they will reject me, if I try to do anything I will fail.
- Critical incident(s): Separation of parents at age 8. Father's re-marriage and birth of half-sister. Difficulties with peer relationships and verbal bullying in school were the final triggers to the school non-attendance. Critical incidents for Emma are likely to be around rejection and loss.
- Negative automatic thoughts:

   ○ **self:** I'm useless, a failure, I have no friends, I'm ugly
   ○ **future:** nothing can ever go right for me, I've wrecked my life, I will be alone forever, nobody will ever understand me
   ○ **world:** everyone hates me, everything I try goes wrong, school is terrible, I have no friends, the world is a depressing place with no hope anywhere.

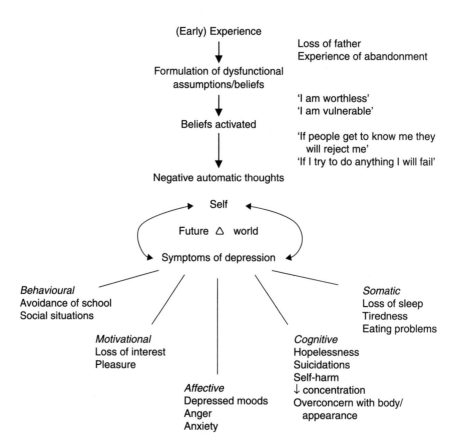

Figure 3.4 Cognitive model of depression: Emma

Formulation summary

Emma is predisposed to becoming depressed by a family history of depression in both parents and being temperamentally 'difficult', that is, demanding, stubborn and always very clinging toward her mother. She has a long history of school non-attendance and a conflicted relationship with her mother who was not able to assert strong boundaries and acknowledged that Emma was able to do much as she pleased over the time of her divorce. Emma was neglected by her father. The older sisters had kept in touch with him but Emma blamed him for leaving and has had very little contact, tending to take her mother's side. Her father therefore rarely acknowledged her at all. Maintaining factors are her isolation, her mother's unavailability and own difficulties and the many longstanding cognitive symptoms of her depressive disorder. In the past, Emma had been given a trial of antidepressant medication by her family doctor that caused unpleasant side effects. She stopped the medication and was very angry that it had not helped.

Strengths: Emma was very bright, imaginative and creative. She was thoughtful and insightful. She could be assertive and held strong opinions. She took much care over her appearance.

It is important that the formulation is at an appropriate level for the young person. The young person needs to be able to understand it and it needs to provide a good understanding of their experiences. It is also unlikely that all elements of the formulation will be evident at this stage, particularly some of the more specific cognitive elements. The clinician should start working with the parts that make sense for the young person. If the hypotheses are not supported when tested then the clinician will need to revise the formulation. The exercise must be genuinely collaborative with the young person and their family.

The family play an important part of the process. The clinician may wish to include aspects of the behaviour of parents and siblings that contribute to maintaining the presenting problems and may also identify cognitive distortions in parents and carers that appear to contribute to the problem and its development. This is discussed further in Chapter 9.

Using formulation in treatment planning

A treatment plan will be constructed around the formulation. It is important to have some early success. This will help the young person feel better, improve engagement and reduce cognitions about hopelessness. Starting with a relatively undemanding task such as activity scheduling will be useful. Formulations also help to set the pace as the clinician gains insight into the young person's level of psychological awareness. This will also provide information as to the best way to present ideas and techniques and whether more creative or non-verbal techniques are required.

The clinician may be able to foresee likely problems in treatment from the conceptualisation, bearing in mind that depressive symptoms can have undermined previous attempts at treatment. This may provide a deeper understanding that results in effective engagement and collaboration.

It is important that there is a shared understanding of the young person's current problems. Initially the young person needs to be aware of how their depression has created everyday problems in their thoughts, feelings and behaviour. This is addressed early on in sharing the formulation. The next level of cognitive work will look at their underlying beliefs that maintain the problems.

Formulations: key points

Formulation and diagnosis of depression are not the same. Formulations provide an explanation of how symptoms have developed and the factors that have had an influence on that development. The diagnosis is a description of symptoms as part of a diagnostic classification systems (ICD-10 or DSM-IV).

The formulation process creates understanding between the young person, family and the clinician. It is based on a hypothesis that is flexible and open to change. It involves sharing information and working collaboratively. It will give guidance on selecting techniques and interventions and reveal likely gaps in information.

In sharing a formulation it is useful to start with specific problems or symptoms. It may be useful to start at the critical incident. The clinician should be careful about contributing their own assumptions and be open and questioning in style, linking theory to practice.

Formulation changes in its aims at different stages of the therapy. In the initial sessions it involves engaging the young person and parents in working collaboratively. It gives a starting point and checks out understanding of the problem as well as creating prioritised goals. In the middle of therapy, formulation helps to recheck if the clinician is on track so that adjustments can be made and any difficulties anticipated and addressed. At this stage cognitive elements are likely to become more evident. At the end of therapy the clinician should have a completed map that makes sense of the young person's experiences. It can also identify vulnerabilities and unsolved problems or areas they may wish to address in the future.

> Formulation tips:
>
> * be curious
> * be careful not to make assumptions
> * the process develops and is elaborated throughout therapy.

4

Starting therapy

Previous chapters have outlined the nature of depression, the theoretical basis for cognitive behaviour therapy (CBT) and the importance of a detailed assessment drawing on information from multiple sources. Assessment continues with psycho-education about depression and development of a CBT formulation.

Figure 4.1 represents an overview of a CBT programme. The first phase of any CBT programme will be a continuation of the assessment, 'Starting CBT' (1–2 sessions); the middle 'treatment phase' can draw from a range of cognitive, behavioural and social problem-solving techniques; and the final 'ending' phase (1 to 4 sessions) concludes therapy. As part of ending, the need for further acute treatment or follow-up and maintenance treatment will need to be considered. The three phases of treatment will be discussed in turn. This chapter addresses the first phase. A clinician prompt sheet is included in the Materials and worksheets.

Engaging young people in therapy

In CBT the clinician and client collaborate using empirical methods to resolve specific problems. The essence of the therapeutic relationship has been described as 'collaborative empiricism'. The clinician empowers, educates and facilitates. The nature of the relationship is inherently attractive to young people who find relating with authority figures resonant with difficulties that they have in relationships with parents and teachers.

Perceived lack of control is often a factor in depression. From the first meeting the clinician takes a friendly, neutral and interested approach placing the young person at the centre of the assessment and optimising their opportunities to contribute to and appropriately influence interactions.

Assessment
Psycho-education
CBT formulation

Starting CBT
List problems and identify goals
Self-monitoring

Middle 'treatment' phase
Cognitive techniques
Behavioural techniques
Social problem-solving
Specific focused interventions

Re-evaluation of goals/reappraisal

Ending therapy

Figure 4.1   Overview of cognitive behaviour therapy (CBT)

This is particularly important if the young person is uncommunicative when allowing worried parents or accompanying professionals to dominate the interview can inhibit engaging the young person. The young person should be talked to first and the context of the assessment explained, including exploring the young person's expectations from the appointment. The clinician might ask the young person who is best situated to inform the therapist about problems. The clinician can request the young person's permission to ask parents and check with the young person whether they agree with how a parent has described a situation and if there is anything that they want to add.

There is a developing theoretical and research interest in the concept of therapeutic alliance and in defining those key interactional factors in the clinician–client relationship that maximise effectiveness (Green, 2006). Successful engagement of depressed young people is widely recognised as a challenge in clinical services. In a recent meta-analysis of published studies of the therapeutic alliance in child mental health services (Shirk and Karver, 2003), ratings of alliance had a consistent but modest effect on treatment outcome. The nature of the problem (internalising versus externalising disorder) was the only moderating variable that produced reliable differences, indicating that the therapeutic alliance is particularly important for young people with externalising disorders such as antisocial behaviour. It is common for depressed young people to have co-morbid antisocial behaviour problems. Research from the USA identifies alliance problems in working with adolescents where there is client hostility, clients with more interpersonal problems, where clients have adverse peer influences and where a history of abuse raises difficulties in early sessions (Shirk, 2002). It is important to attend to the adolescent's experience, present the clinician as an ally and formulate personally meaningful goals for the young person.

Shirk identified four different treatment engagement strategies that can be useful for hard to reach populations:

- experience focused ('lots of young people that I have seen have told me about similar problems at home')
- motivation focused ('this is going to be hard work but if we work together . . .')
- negotiation focused ('maybe we could give this a try?')
- efficacy based interventions ('lots of young people that I have seen tell me that they have found this helpful').

During therapy, alliance has been categorised into personal alliance, the 'therapeutic relationship', and task alliance, consisting of the clinician clearly working with the client on the client's goals with both being important in outcome. It is not only important that the young person rates the clinician positively but also that the clinician and client have shared goals.

A further framework that has related to engagement is motivational interviewing. This is based on a model of behaviour change that starts with the assumption that people do not make simple decisions to change problem behaviours but that there are a succession of stages involved (Prochaska and Diclemente, 1982). Clinical intervention therefore needs to be tailored to the individual's stage of change. At first the individual may be in a precontemplation stage where they do not think that there is a problem. In the contemplation stage the individual is ambivalent and is able to evaluate the pros and cons of change. In the preparation stage planning starts and in the action stage the young person makes specific changes towards goals. Once change is achieved the individual moves into a maintenance stage. It seems that there are two components underlying readiness to change. These are not only accepting that there is a problem or willingness to change (importance) but also a belief that one can effect change (confidence). Consideration of these two dimensions can help the clinician support the young person in engaging with CBT. A lack of perception of importance might be addressed by providing more information; a lack of confidence by highlighting other areas where the young person has taken something on successfully.

Motivational interviewing was developed from work with substance misusing adults, and has detailed successful techniques to address the early stages of the change process. It is a client-centred directive method for enhancing motivation to change by exploring and resolving ambivalence (Miller and Rollnik, 2002). It is not based on any specific therapeutic model but is a combination of style and technique. In summary, the basic principles are of reflective listening and acceptance of the young person's perspective while examining alternatives in an open-minded way. It can involve recognition of the difficulties involved in change and recognising that symptoms can have a protective function.

> *Rob age 16 was referred by his youth offending team worker. He was estranged from his family and living most of the time at a friend's flat. He had recent offences for shoplifting. He had been depressed since his parents' separation and being rejected by each of them in succession several months earlier. His lifestyle was chaotic, lacking any routines and he no longer had contact with a stable social network. He expressed very negative feelings about himself and the future but attended for the session following an initial meeting. He could see little purpose in any therapy, feeling that everything was hopeless. The clinician focused on listening to his perceptions of his difficulties, a number of which were complex practical issues. The clinician's initial aim was to continue a dialogue about the possibility of positive change, asking open questions and reflecting on the answers with an equal balance of power with Rob, affirming and acknowledging difficulties. Rob was supported in recognising that he had some choices. Over several sessions including some cancellations Rob and the clinician worked to identify some small achievable goals in addressing his problems, considering options and areas of potential difficulty and risks of negative outcomes. This began with making contact with his older sister, getting some help with his financial situation and looking into a part-time college access course.*

Key factors in engagement:

- work from the young person's perspective
- be prepared to take time
- reflective listening.

The first sessions: introducing the young person to CBT

The introduction of the rationale and components of CBT to the young person is crucial in engaging them. The young person needs to decide actively that they want to try this particular form of treatment. There are a number of areas to cover and it may be helpful to ask them to think over the offer of treatment and to decide if they definitely want to give it a try after hearing what is entailed. Leaflets explaining CBT and depression are useful for both parents and young people (see Materials and worksheets).

Introduction to therapy: young people

- Acknowledge participation.
- Collaborative working.
- Home practice.
- Structure of treatment.
- Confidentiality.
- Rationale for CBT and psycho-education.

Acknowledge participation

The young person has chosen to participate in CBT to 'work on their problems'. Acknowledge the young person's involvement and joint responsibility with the clinician for working on their difficulties.

- 'Well done for deciding that you want to try this treatment.'
- 'There is no magic solution to most problems but if you really want to change things about your life and the way things are, this treatment gives you an opportunity to try.'
- 'Shall we give it a try?'

Collaborative working

CBT is a brief problem-solving treatment. It is based on collaboration with the young person and clinician working towards agreed goals.

- 'This treatment will mean that at the beginning we agree what the main problems are and together get to understand them better and try out different ways of helping. It is teamwork.'

Home practice

Clinicians are often concerned that raising the issue of 'homework' will discourage young people who will have negative associations with the word from school. It is therefore particularly important that they understand the purpose of tasks set during each session.

- 'Every week we will be working on particular things to tackle the problems that we have talked about. Together we will work out how you can put things into practice at home and come back to talk about how you have got on at the next session. This helps us to understand the problems better because I only see you for a short time each week and this means that you can practise and experiment with the work we do in the sessions.'

Structure of treatment

This involves explaining to the young person the nature of the commitment to the therapy.

- 'The therapy consists of about 12 sessions in total. We can arrange the sessions after school so that you don't miss out on your work. Each session lasts about 45 minutes and there will be some homework each week. It is important to finish the therapy once you have started. What we usually do is have a review of how things are going after three sessions to make sure that we are making progress. If you are not finding it helpful then we can think again. Is that ok?'

It is useful to set the times of the first three sessions with the young person on the first meeting. These will need to take place at least weekly. It is very difficult to sustain therapy with gaps between sessions longer than a week, particularly at the early stages of relationship building and familiarising the young person with the therapeutic approach. Further detail of the organisation of sessions can be explained:

- 'Usually what we will do is start off with seeing how you have been getting on since the last session. We will look at any home practice then work on the topic for that week.'

Confidentiality

This is an important area for any psychotherapeutic work with young people and it is essential at the beginning of CBT to define the boundaries of the treatment and involvement of parents or carers in the sessions. For the therapy to be most effective, the clinician needs to be allied with the young person from the young person's point of view and to be allied with the parents from their point of view. It will be necessary to include parents or carers in the therapeutic programme in most cases. This must be explained clearly at the outset and the young person will need to agree with the planned approach.

- 'The sessions will be mainly spent just with you. The things we talk about will be confidential, if there are things which I feel it necessary to share with your parents then I will tell you first. It will be important for me to talk with you and your parents together about every other session to see how things are going and how they can help. When we have our review, I think it would be a good idea for us all to meet together for at least part of it.'

It is good practice to include the young person in sessions with their parents. It is important to be clear with parents how any contact outside the session, for instance telephone call or messages from them before the young person attends will be handled. In general the young person will be told about the telephone call. Issues in working with parents are discussed in more detail in Chapter 9.

Rationale for CBT and psycho-education

The basis for the therapeutic approach needs to be explained during the initial sessions. This may include explanation of the common symptoms of depression, normalising the young person's experience of symptoms and linking the symptoms into a cognitive behavioural explanation. The explanation needs to be targeted to the understanding of the young person. The clinician will need to define cognitions: 'thoughts, ideas and beliefs are circulating inside our heads all the time. They affect our behaviour'. Continue with an explanation of the therapeutic process. 'These thoughts affect how we feel. When people feel down and depressed they are often thinking bad thoughts about themselves (I'm hopeless and useless), about the future (nothing's going to change) and the world (everything always goes wrong, everyone hates me). Treatment works towards identifying these negative thoughts, understanding them better and changing them.' 'You'll understand this better as we work through the treatment. Have you ever done anything like this before?'

It is often helpful to establish early on the young person's understanding of certain key terms, particularly recognising symptoms of depression. For example, what does the young person understand by the terms 'hopeless' or 'concentration'? The quality of the description often gives useful clues about their ability to describe these symptoms in the context of therapy.

Introducing the young person to therapy includes clarifying:

- how the clinician plans to work with the young person
- what is depression and how CBT works for depressive symptoms
- structure of sessions and home practice.

Introduction to therapy/psycho-education: parents and carers

Key points about depression and CBT also need to be explained to parents. The extent of parental involvement will be determined by the age of the young person, the nature of their difficulties and the young person's relationship with their parents. For carers who are not parents, similar principles will be involved but these may vary according to the nature of the carers' responsibilities. As for young people, explanatory leaflets can be helpful.

Introduction to therapy: parents

- Aims of therapy.
- Rationale of therapy.
- Outline of therapy.
- Expectation of progress.
- Confidentiality.
- Parental involvement.

Aims of therapy

The expressed aims of therapy will clearly be targeted to the needs of particular parents.

- 'The treatment is aimed at helping young people to understand why they feel bad or depressed and to be able to change this. It is focused on mood and feelings although there may be other problems identified by the young person which they wish to work on.'

Rationale of therapy

As for the young person, explanations need to be targeted towards the understanding and experience of the parents. An explanation of the rationale of cognitive therapy is usually helpful in gaining parents' confidence and positive expectations of therapy. It may be useful to outline evidence from research and clinical experience of the efficacy of CBT to further reinforce parental collaboration.

Outline of therapy

Length of treatment and timing of appointments will need to be discussed with some attention to the practicalities of the young person attending. Weekly sessions are needed at first to maintain the momentum of therapy and there may be a need to meet twice weekly initially if symptoms are severe. Sessions normally last 45 minutes. Parents need to know about their involvement in the therapy. It is helpful if they can attend for at least alternate appointments to give feedback on progress and support with the programme. They need to be told that the young person will have homework and a diary to complete and that their help may be needed as part of the programme.

Expectation of progress

A summary of expectations and contingencies for a worsening of the young person's condition should be given.

- 'It is our experience with the treatment that most will improve but that this may take several sessions. Improvement may be gradual or progress may be "up and down". If you are worried feel free to contact me. We find that attending for a complete course is essential for improvement to be maintained, even if things start to improve quite quickly at the beginning. I suggest that we all meet together after two (for example) sessions to review progress.'

Confidentiality

Parents may have some anxieties about their son or daughter engaging in individual treatment and may feel threatened and undermined by a developing therapeutic relationship. It is important to reassure them of the boundaries of this relationship and of the confidentiality agreement with the young person. It is often helpful to say when and how they will have opportunities to speak with you to discuss progress.

Parental involvement

It is important at the outset to negotiate appropriate parental involvement. The usual level would consist of the parent joining the end of each or alternate sessions with the young person for the final 10–15 minutes. The minimum would be a review including the parent at the initial assessment after the fourth session, and at the completion of the programme. More extended sessions with the family as a whole or with the young person and parents together may be appropriate for some situations.

> Parents need to be involved actively but the space for work with the young person individually needs to be created with clear boundaries about communication with the clinician.

Identifying goals of treatment

Cognitive therapy is a collaborative exercise between the clinician and young person with an emphasis on clear agendas and goals for therapy. Identification of goals takes place following the initial assessment and is a crucial stage of the engagement process.

> Identifying goals of treatment:
>
> * identify problems
> * rate severity of problems
> * translate problems into target symptoms
> * agreement on three to four goals of treatment.

Identify problems

Young people often will have a different perspective on problems from their parents or carers. It is important that information from either source is not treated as strictly factual and hence that conflicting information implies that one source is distorting the truth.

It is often helpful to ask: 'What are the things about yourself, your life and the way you get on with other people that you would like to change?' Once the young person has made a start, a collaborative approach can be used to negotiate achievable goals. Using the example of Emma from Chapter 3:

Therapist: *What are the things about yourself, your life and the way you get on with other people that you would like to change?*

Emma: *Everything! I hate the way I look, I hate my mum and I want to go to a new school.*

Therapist: *OK. There are some problems that we can work on together with this therapy and there are some problems that it is not possible to change, like your appearance. What we can work on though is the way you feel about yourself. Is that a problem for you?*

Emma: *Yes, most of the time I hate myself and feel useless.*

Therapist: *Is that about your self-confidence? That is the sort of problem that we might work on together.*

Emma: *Yes, my self-confidence is a big problem for me.*

Therapist: *Can you tell me any ways that your self-confidence makes things difficult?*

Emma: *My mum says to me that I give up things too easily if they are hard.*

Therapist: *You said that your relationship with your mum gets you down.*

Emma: *Yes, I feel very sad about what's going wrong between us and about other things too like school.*

Therapist: *Would you like to feel less down and depressed and to work on that as a problem?*

Emma: *Yes.*

Therapist: *OK, we've got two important problems now. Are there any other areas say for example the way you get on with your friends?*

Emma: *(thinks) I do have friends but we have a lot of arguments and I lose my temper and end up not speaking to them*

Therapist: *Do you think that your temper is a problem for you?*

Emma: *(laughs) Yes. I'm always getting into trouble for it . . .*

Translating problems into target symptoms

Ideally, the focus of the therapeutic intervention should be at a symptom level.

The problems identified may be linked in with commonly recognised features of depression, which can be broken down into the following categories:

1   mood symptoms: sadness, anger
2   motivational: everything too much effort, apathy
3   cognitive: poor concentration, hopelessness, suicidal thoughts
4   behaviour: social withdrawal, arguments, school avoidance
5   physical symptoms: sleep and appetite disturbance.

Emma and the clinician determine the symptoms which are most distressing and most amenable to treatment. It is helpful to list the problems together on a sheet of paper. The identification of problems helps determine the emphasis of future therapy sessions. The young person may include problems on the problem list that will not be directly addressed in therapy for instance a problem related to parental behaviour such as that a parent drinks too much. These should be acknowledged and listed. The clinician may emphasise that the therapy will focus on some but not all difficulties but that feeling better generally helps tackle life problems more positively.

Rating of severity of problem areas

It is a useful exercise to ask the young person to rate each identified problem for severity on a 1 to 10-point scale at the outset. Using a visual scale (see Materials and worksheets) can be helpful, explaining that 1 is 'ok' and 10 is 'the worst ever'. Ratings highlight for the clinician the relative importance of each and will help in setting an agenda for therapy. In addition it offers a crude method of assessing progress. It is useful to outline to young people that at the review meeting, half way through therapy, it will be helpful to re-score the problems to see if there has been any improvement.

Example of Emma's problem list

Problem	Rating
1 Difficulty getting on with my mum.	9
2 Feeling bad about myself.	8
3 Getting depressed.	7
4 Losing my temper with my friends.	5
5 Hate school.	5

Agreement on goals of treatment

Problems are translated into goals by the clinician and young person identifying a positive statement about how things could be in the future that is incompatible with the problem area (see the goal list below). When goals of therapy have been negotiated, the young person is again encouraged to write them down in their own words, facilitating ownership of the process. One goal should involve depressed mood. Goals could be:

- 'Feel less depressed'
- 'Get on better with friends'
- 'Find ways to tell people how I feel without being angry'
- 'Enjoy myself doing things and feel less bored'.

It is important to avoid goals that are outside the control of the young person or are unrealistic for instance to lose weight. It can be helpful to ask the young person how they might know that things have improved or what the first sign of improvement might be.

Example of Emma's goal list

1 Getting on better with my mum,
   enjoying doing nice things together.
2 Feeling better about myself.
3 Not getting depressed.
4 Be able to say what I think.

List problems, paying attention to symptoms of depression, then use these to define positive outcomes to be worked on as goals.

Clinicians re-appraisal

At the completion of this stage, the clinician needs to draw together the information obtained to plan the treatment programme. Chapter 11 outlines common problems encountered at this stage of therapy with suggestions for how to resolve them. Below are some important questions to consider in order to plan the following sessions of the programme.

Clinician re-appraisal: six important questions to ask

1   *How severe is the depression?* This is a key question throughout the assessment and the clinician will have considered the need for intensive treatment, for instance inpatient admission and urgent attention to the young person's safety. It is important to consider which symptoms are currently most handicapping. For young people who have no motivation and pronounced sleep impairment, monitoring and scheduling activities together with teaching sleep hygiene measures will be needed (see Chapter 5). Some young people will be pre-occupied by distressing images and intrusive thoughts (possibly of suicide) and it will be important to give the young person techniques for dealing with these early on. Equally, there may be environmental factors to do with school or the family that need to be addressed possibly outside of the individual treatment.

2   *Assessing suicidal thoughts.* In work with young people with mood disturbance it is always important to consider and evaluate the risk of self-harming behaviour. Suicidal thoughts can be difficult to talk about and many worry that it may not be safe to open up the subject with young people. However, the evidence shows that open discussion causes no harm. On the contrary, many suicidal young people experience a real sense of relief when they are given the opportunity to talk about their distressing feelings. Risk assessment is discussed in more detail in Chapter 10.

3   *What problems are currently most distressing to the young person?* Identification of goals of therapy will have highlighted priorities for the young person. It is essential to work on problems that young people perceive as relevant to their immediate concerns. Where there is potential disagreement between clinician and young person about priorities, discussion of the advantages and disadvantages of each option can help in drawing up a mutually satisfactory plan. Disagreement can arise over problems such as 'being overweight' or self-harm. In the first instance the depressed young person may need to be dissuaded from trying to lose weight before working on his or her depressed mood. In the second instance the young person may require help in seeing that self-harm is a problem which may be amenable to treatment.

4   *What problem is currently most open to change?* To encourage hope and foster engagement in treatment, it is crucial to facilitate successful

experiences early on in the therapy. Therefore in prioritising problems, it is helpful to work on a simple solvable problem first. Young people can then attribute this success to themselves and gain an experience of being in control. For adolescents who are severely depressed, it may be important to enlist parents' active assistance. It is important to analyse the young person's repertoire of coping skills and their support networks.

5   *Does the young person have the cognitive maturity to use all elements of CBT?* By working through a detailed assessment the clinician will gain a clear idea of how well the young person will be able to use cognitive techniques. A degree of insight and the ability to self-monitor is essential for this. For young people who find detecting negative automatic thoughts and describing and differentiating emotional states difficult, an emphasis on simple cognitive techniques, behavioural techniques and social problem-solving will be most helpful. For young people who immediately respond to an explanation of depressive symptoms involving linking automatic thoughts with emotional states, a predominantly cognitive approach is likely to be possible.

6   *Is the young person ready for therapy?* How has the young person responded to the treatment rationale so far? Have they elected to give CBT a try? How far is the young person able to form a collaborative relationship? Forces within the young person's family, social or educational system may be posing challenges for the efficacy of therapy. In some instances, issues of blame and grievance may be mitigating against engagement. Both the young person, the family and any other agencies need to be at a stage to start a treatment programme.

Home practice

The importance of home practice as a part of treatment has been mentioned above. It may be useful to start with a recording task at home at the first goal-setting session. The clinician should start with a small assignment at first and gradually increase requirements as appropriate. Different tasks will be developed according to session content. The principle is to ensure some home practice between all sessions. Below is a summary of practical aspects.

1   *Introduction of the diary and homework.* A diary (notebook or loose leaf file) is given to the young person as early in the programme as is practical. They are encouraged to make it more personal by writing their name on it and decorating it. It is explained that it is important for the young person to keep a record of certain thoughts/feelings/events between the sessions and that this will help both young person and clinician to think together about what has been happening and how things could improve further.

2   *Setting up the home practice.* It is very important that this is done carefully. All home practice must be related to the session context and

develop as a natural consequence of the work of the session and be developed as collaboratively as possible ('Can you think of a way that you could try that out at home?'). The young person needs to have clear instructions about what to do, and to be made aware of how central practice is to each session. It is helpful for the clinician to write the instructions in the diary, using clear, simple language and pitched at the level appropriate for the young person's literacy skills. It is important to emphasise that spelling and presentation style is not important in any written records, unlike school work. Before closing the session, the clinician checks that the young person has understood by asking them to explain what they need to do before the next session. Starting the assignment in the session can be helpful. Sometimes it is helpful to decide beforehand when a task might be tried out or a mood record made and prompts arranged.

3   *Home practice review.* The home practice review is an important part of the session as it links the themes of the previous session with those of the current one. The clinician should comment positively. It may also be appropriate, with the young person's permission, to write positive comments in the diary. By positively reinforcing the young person's work with the diary, the clinician is:

- reinforcing the concept of reward, which is an important theme running through the therapy
- giving the message that the young person can do something positive to help themselves.

If the young person has either not completed the diary or has not brought it to the session, it is important to give a clear message that it would have been preferable if they had completed the task, as this would have given the clinician a better understanding of how the young person has been feeling recently. In these circumstances the clinician will want to find out sensitively any reasons why the young person did not do the homework. For instance, the clinician may not have been clear enough about the task or the young person felt too depressed to do it. Positive reinforcement is important, otherwise home practice may become yet another source of feelings of worthlessness and failure.

Specific points relating to review of homework tasks are included after the homework instructions for each session. The clinician will need to check these in preparation for the following session. In Chapter 11 there is further discussion on troubleshooting homework problems.

Starting CBT:

- the young person must actively decide to try CBT
- a key task in introducing CBT to the young person is engagement in collaborative working

- the structure, rationale and degree of commitment to CBT must be outlined

- it is helpful if parents are engaged in the treatment programme. The amount of involvement will vary for each individual

- goals must be negotiated that are positive, achievable and measurable

- following the first two sessions, the clinician must re-appraise the young person's symptoms and plan the central part of the treatment package.

5

Early stages of therapy

The early stages of cognitive behaviour therapy (CBT) include helping the young person label their feelings, link feelings to situations, recognise depressed behaviour and start to activate themselves. The next step is to recognise the thoughts that are associated with the feelings that they experience. Techniques of emotional recognition, activity scheduling and self-monitoring are involved and it is also helpful to focus on managing sleep problems early in therapy.

> The initial stages of CBT focus upon the following tasks:
>
> * emotional recognition
> * activity scheduling
> * managing sleep problems
> * self-monitoring.

Emotional recognition

Emotional recognition, referred to as affective education by some authors, involves identifying words used to describe emotions. Young people are helped to recognise and label their emotions, to distinguish between different emotions, to differentiate feelings and thoughts and to recognise links between feelings and events. The clinician can ensure that they are using a shared vocabulary and communicating effectively with the young person. This session provides a relevant start to exploring depressed mood and serves to further engage the young person. The session also introduces the distinction between feelings and thoughts, enabling further assessment of the ease with which the adolescent will respond to a cognitive approach. The young person learns to observe their own feelings. A clinician prompt sheet is included in the Materials and worksheets.

Rationale

1 The young person may use different words from the clinician or have a restricted vocabulary for description of emotional states.
2 Depressed young people may have difficulties in identifying their own or other people's emotions.
3 They may have difficulty in distinguishing between different types of emotions for instance anger and irritability.
4 Depressed young people tend to perceive their feelings as being out of their control. The opportunity to define and identify the way they feel, as well as linking it to their thoughts and situations, often helps them to feel less helpless and more in control of their mood.

Emotional recognition involves:

- defining different emotions
- distinguishing between different emotional states
- self-monitoring
- linking emotions with cognitions and events.

Defining different emotions

Emotional recognition cards may be used for this session. Names of emotions can be written on separate cards that are given to the young person to read one at a time. Although cards may be more obviously suitable for younger age groups, they provide a focus for conversation with adolescents who may have problems with both social and emotional aspects of communication.

Emotions that can be used include:

- ashamed
- confused
- mixed up
- irritable
- excited
- frustrated
- guilty

- happy
- hurt
- left out
- calm
- lonely
- angry
- sad
- unhappy
- scared
- upset
- disappointed.

The young person is asked to describe each feeling in as much detail as possible because people use different words for feelings and it is important for the clinician to check. They are asked to give a recent example of the emotion on the card, describing how that feeling is for them and if they can remember a situation when they felt that way. For instance they could be asked to imagine that they had to explain the meaning of that word to someone who had never felt that way. The clinician should reassure them that this is a difficult task, use positive reinforcement and prompt liberally. It is sometimes possible to elicit cognitions at the same time although this is not the principal aim of the task. The cards can be presented in groups, for example, 'sad' 'unhappy', 'upset', 'hurt' can be presented together, as can 'happy' and 'excited'. The following dialogue illustrates this process.

Therapist: *Have a go at describing how it feels to be sad or unhappy. Try to describe the feeling so that someone who had never felt like that might understand.*

Young person: *It's very difficult to put it into words . . .*

Therapist: *Is it a good feeling?*

Young person: *No, it's bad. You feel slow and like you can't be bothered to do anything and haven't got any energy. It sort of hurts inside and makes you tense . . .*

Therapist: *You are very good at describing sadness. Tell me about the last time you felt like that.*

Young person: *Last night.*

Therapist: *Can you tell me exactly when you started to feel unhappy, where you were and what you were doing?*

Young person: *It started when I went upstairs to get ready for bed, and got really bad when I tried to go to sleep.*

Therapist: *I wonder if you can remember any more about that? What thoughts were going round inside your head when you started to feel sad.*

Young person: *I was thinking about school, how I couldn't face it, how worried I am about my mum and dad and blaming myself for making everything worse . . .*

Although the aim of the session and the therapy tasks are the same, the approach and the way the session is introduced to each young person will vary according to age and maturity. With younger adolescents, the clinician relies more on the use of the cards, attempting to engage them through an activity-based approach. In contrast, the clinician can rely more on verbal communication with older adolescents. Older adolescents have greater facility in defining emotions and might therefore be offended if the clinician tries to engage them by putting too much emphasis on the cards. It is important to strike a balance between making unwarranted assumptions about the young person's emotional vocabulary and risking infantilisation. For young people who have difficulty with finding an example from their own experience, using situations involving other people or characters from film or television may be helpful.

Distinguishing between emotional states

The use of the emotional recognition cards allows comparisons to be made between emotions. Most young people understand that moods are often not 'pure'. There can be a close relationship between 'anger' and 'depression'. It is therefore useful to check whether they can make the distinction. If there is some difficulty in labelling, the use of further examples can help to separate out emotional states.

Some young people may have difficulty in understanding that feelings and thoughts are not the same. In this case the remainder of this session should concentrate on recognition and verbalisation of emotions. For young people who have a wide emotional vocabulary that they are able to communicate, the distinction between mood, activity and thoughts can be introduced by a general statement such as 'When we feel sad or happy, certain thoughts may be crossing our mind'.

Mood ratings

Young people are asked to rate the severity of their moods or feelings on a ten-point scale. A visual scale is included in the Materials and worksheets with 1 representing the lowest mood. This technique assists with self-monitoring and is useful throughout therapy.

Home practice

The home practice task for this session involves continuing work with linking emotions with events and cognitions. The clinician explains that it is important for the young person to keep a record of events and feelings between sessions. This will help both the young person and clinician to think together about what has been happening between the sessions and will help the clinician to connect the therapy session with everyday life for the young person. The first task is to keep a daily record of moods and feelings. This task continues the work started in the session. It may be useful to divide each page of the diary into three columns, headed 'What I was doing'; 'feelings'; and 'What I was thinking' (see Materials and worksheets). The task is to describe at least one mood or feeling occurring each day with an emphasis on low mood states. The clinician should work an example in the diary to act as a model.

If the young person had difficulty identifying cognitions, the homework task can be limited to the daily identification of feelings and their association with events or activities. Some young people will be finding it difficult at this stage to distinguish between feelings and thoughts and therefore fall back on answers such as 'I don't know', 'I don't remember', or repeat an emotional state (such as feeling sad) instead of describing a thought. Time taken to give detailed descriptions of what is required will be well spent. Continuous prompting reinforces the idea that mood, events and thoughts are different. Despite the clinician's positive reinforcement, the young person might not be able to complete the full task at this stage.

Thomas (aged 12) described feeling very low in mood and losing interest in all his friends over a 3-month period. Important factors in his depression were his parents' frequent arguments and threats of separation; his best friend leaving school and his mother being chronically ill. After the emotional recognition session Thomas completed the following entry in his diary (Table 5.1), using the three column chart.

Table 5.1 Thomas' diary entries

What was happening/ what I was doing	What I was feeling (rating 1–10 with 1 best and 10 worst)	What I was thinking
In playground at school	Sad 7/10	I've got no friends
Standing on my own	Lonely 10/10	I'll never have any friends
	Worried 5/10	Nobody likes me
		I'm all alone

Darryl (aged 13) was not very articulate and had some learning difficulties at school. He found it difficult to define different emotional states, although he was interested in the card task. He looked very pleased with himself when he was able to describe an emotional state in his own words. He was prompted to give an example if he struggled to describe how he felt. The more concrete task was easier for him and he again looked pleased when he found an example (such as, confused: 'I feel confused when my mother tells me different things and I don't know what I am supposed to do').

It was difficult for Darryl to think of what he was doing at the time of being in a certain emotional state. Events seemed to be inseparable from his mood. Talking about thoughts was even more difficult. When asked, he said that 'feelings and thoughts are the same thing'.

Despite this claim, the clinician continued. Darryl eventually made an important link between mood, events and thoughts during their practice:

Therapist: Could you remember the last time that you felt sad?
Darryl: Last night.
Therapist: What were you doing when you were feeling sad?
Darryl: I was lying in bed.
Therapist: What were you thinking about at the time?
Long pause. The question was repeated twice.
Darryl: I was thinking of my dad.

This was an important link as he was relating for the first time his depressed mood with a life event (his father's serious illness). Darryl was pleased when he was given a diary with his name on the cover. He said that he had never been given a diary before.

Donna (aged 12) presented with depressive symptoms, psychosomatic complaints and school non-attendance. During the assessment inter-view, she was tearful and complained of abdominal pain. She gave little information about herself, most of her answers being 'I don't know!'

During the first session of therapy, she was very compliant and appeared relaxed. She looked surprised when the clinician asked her to describe different emotions. She soon realised what she was being asked to do and appeared to enjoy the rest of the session.

Donna had a good understanding of the emotional terms and seemed able to distinguish between mood and thoughts. Her main dif-ficulty was in recalling examples of different emotional states that she had experienced recently. The clinician prompted her by asking her to think of a girl of the same age. She then asked her to think of this girl feeling sad, angry or happy. This was followed by questions such as 'What is this girl doing when she feels sad?', or 'What is this girl thinking when she feels sad?' Donna found this approach much easier and she immediately related to this 'imaginary friend'. She provided descriptions such as 'She is sad because she is teased by other kids at school', or 'When she is sad, she thinks that she is fat and ugly'. This 'projective' technique not only helped her to participate in the session but she also started making spontaneous causal links between event, mood and thoughts.

Paul (aged 14) had complex problems, including depressive symptoms, conduct disorder and drug misuse. During the period of therapy, he was voluntarily admitted to a young people's residential unit as a result of conflict with his parents.

His poor peer relationships and low self-esteem emerged as themes during the practice with the emotional vocabulary. He felt left out at school during physical education because the other boys made personal negative comments. He also felt inferior because he did not have any trainers or appropriate equipment. This situation resulted in depressed mood and self-blaming thoughts.

Home practice review: emotional recognition

Once into therapy all sessions begin with a general review of how the past week has been, followed by a review of home practice. At the conclusion of the emotional recognition session the young person was asked to record some examples of events and, for some, thoughts that are linked with specific feelings. The clinician should take a position of interested enquiry during which they highlight the mood–thought–events links.

Many depressed young people present with anxiety symptoms and irritability. It is important to discuss incidents when the young person felt anxious or angry.

The young person is then encouraged to describe the three columns of the diary in more detail, i.e. what they were feeling and thinking, as well as what was happening.

The young person can be prompted to expand on brief answers such as 'I was thinking of my mother'. Facilitating questions include 'Can you remember what were you actually worried about' or 'Could you tell me a bit more about your worries at that time?'

If the young person has not completed the diary, the clinician can go through the task with them in the session by asking them to recall recent examples. If the young person gives answers such as 'I do not remember' or 'I do not know', the clinician should keep prompting (e.g. 'Have a good think'). If the young person is still unable to recall recent emotional states, the question could be reversed by asking them to recall recent events which could then lead to the discussion of mood and thoughts.

Activity scheduling

Activity scheduling, referred to as behavioural activation by some authors, is the first strategy in therapy which directly addresses the young person's symptoms. This is often necessary before other problems can be tackled. Depressed young people commonly feel that they have little control over their symptoms and their lives. They will frequently have ceased activities that they have previously enjoyed and become less socially active both at home and at school. They are likely to obtain less enjoyment in general and have little motivation for any activities.

In addition to experiencing fewer pleasurable activities depressed young people are likely to undervalue their own achievement, reinforcing their low self-esteem.

> **Re-activating the young person and breaking the negative cycle of boredom and inactivity is the first step in lifting mood.**

Activity scheduling provides useful information about the young person's functioning in several areas, for instance if they are staying up very late or have a reversed day/night cycle or if they are spending much time on their own. School attendance may be identified as a problem and lack of peer group networks be apparent.

Activity scheduling is a two stage process. The first stage is to obtain detailed information about the young person's activities. The young person is asked to keep a diary (see Materials and worksheets for handout and example diary forms) which involves recording activity during each day, usually on an hour by hour basis from the time they get up until they go to sleep.

A rationale might be provided as follows: 'Young people who are feeling depressed often find that they gradually change their day to day activities. It will help us in working on your problems to get a picture of what you are doing every day. First I would like you to complete a diary for me. Let's fill in the section together about what you did yesterday . . .'

> **Example of activity scheduling:**
>
> | | |
> |---|---|
> | 8.00 | Wake up, get up, get washed and dressed |
> | 8.30 | Breakfast |
> | 9.00 | Watch TV |
> | 10.00 | Visit friend |
> | 12.00 | Eat lunch |
> | 1.30–4.00 | Shopping with friend |
> | 5.00 | Eat tea |
> | 6.00 | Watch TV, homework |
> | 8.00 | Play on computer |
> | 10.00 | Bed |

A clinician prompt sheet is included in the Materials and worksheets.

> The first session of activity scheduling involves linking lack of activity with low mood and starting to keep a record of daily activities.

Scheduling activities

At the following session the activity diary is carefully reviewed. The importance of building in activities that are enjoyable or that give a sense of achievement is introduced. Together the clinician and young person schedule activities in detail for the coming week. Activities over which the young person has some control are chosen. These can be everyday activities, preferably including another person, and should not be special events. The clinician might suggest some activities if the young person has difficulty with this. This could, for example, include phoning a friend, visiting a friend, sports activities, playing a game of cards with a sibling or watching a TV programme with a parent. Some young people have very limited opportunities as a result of losing their social network through prolonged school absence or geographical isolation. Clinicians should remember that the best approach is to start by re-instating previous activities and using home oriented activities at first. Re-introducing activities that were previously experienced positively is often a first step but new activities can also be introduced. It is important that activities start with small steps and are likely to be successful. The programme for the planned activities is written down on the diary for the young person.

A rationale can be presented along the following lines: 'When you are bored and have nothing to do, bad thoughts we have talked about are likely to come into your mind. I want you to do an experiment with me to see whether if you keep yourself busy that you find that you feel better.'

It may be important to elicit parents' or carers' consent for activities that involve spending money or changes in routine. The diary is continued and the new activities recorded alongside other activities. The idea of rewarding yourself for trying new, difficult or avoided activities can be introduced. The clinician is both activating the young person, which will decrease the amount of time spent bored, ruminating, isolated and also increasing reward and pleasure which will increase positive self-talk.

Paul (aged 14) was referred by social services after his voluntary accommodation in a residential unit. This was precipitated by continuing conflict with his parents. He presented with depressive symptoms, suicidal ideation, conduct disorder and drug misuse. He gave a spontaneous account of all the negative events that had occurred during the previous week: 'I did a runner from the home and slashed my wrists on Sunday. It was a terrible week'. At the same time he had kept a detailed diary showing that he had missed school and spent the days and much of the evenings wandering in the park on his own. During the session and in collaboration with his key worker, activities which involved other people were scheduled during each day and a supportive approach taken to his current school non-attendance, with a planned gradual re-integration.

At the second session on activity scheduling the therapist and young person identify activities and programme them into the week ahead. Parents usually need to be involved in supporting this.

Introducing concepts of achievement and pleasure

It is helpful to combine behavioural activation more specifically with the evaluation of enjoyment and sense of achievement derived from activities. It is to be expected that activities rated highest on these dimensions will be most effective in lifting mood. This is particularly useful for young people with low motivation and high levels of social withdrawal. Rating both achievement and pleasure can assist in avoiding the trap that everything should be fun or alternatively that achieving success is all important. The young person can be asked to rate each activity on a scale of 1 to 10 to reflect these dimensions. This may be added into diary recordings at a later stage. With increased activation over time it is anticipated that the young person will rate activities increasingly positively.

Some depressed young people may still be unable to identify anything that gives them pleasure. In this situation, the clinician may need to enquire about rewards that are 'less boring' or that result in the young person feeling 'not as bad' as usual. Describing enjoyment can be difficult for depressed individuals who feel that nothing is pleasurable. The advantage of a rating scale is that small changes in positive (or absence of negative) mood state can be registered. For some this can be used to begin discussion of negative thoughts prompted during periods of low mood.

Finally in activity scheduling the young person learns to link activities with achievement and pleasure.

Rewards for scheduling activities can further assist in lifting mood. Potential rewards may be material or internal. The latter are more difficult to conceptualise and achieve, particularly for younger adolescents. However, the introduction of positive cognitions as self-rewards is essential as it may lead to subsequent work involving a restructure of negative thoughts and beliefs.

Rewards may also be provided by the parent or carer. This is important, as young people may not have full control in achieving certain rewards (for instance inviting a friend home). If self-rewards have implications for the young person's normal routine, it is particularly important that the carer is fully involved in planning and implementation. It may therefore be useful to include the carer in part of the session. If parents have difficulty in viewing rewards as justified then specific intervention with them is likely to be required to discuss and understand their beliefs. It is important that the clinician identifies some rewards that do not require parental involvement. A questionnaire for identifying rewards is included in the Materials and worksheets.

Examples of rewards

Self-rewards

1   Material:
    - having a favourite snack
    - buying an ice-cream/sweet from the nearest shop
    - watching a favourite DVD
    - inviting a friend home.

2   Thoughts:
    - thinking, 'Well done!'
    - thinking, 'I am proud of myself'
    - thinking, 'I am pleased with myself'.

Parents' rewards

1   Material:
    - joining you in a favoured activity at home
    - taking you to a favourite event
    - giving a token towards the purchase of a small gift
    - helping you to visit a close friend.

2   Verbal:
    - phrases such as, 'I am very pleased with you'
    - 'I am glad to see you happy today.' 'Well done!'.

Darryl (aged 13) kept an activity diary showing that he spent almost all of his waking hours when not at school watching TV on his own at home in his room. He said that he would like to be able to go out to the shop on an errand for his mother as something to achieve.

When practice was reviewed, he said that he had gone to the shop and his mother rewarded him by allowing him to buy a magazine. However, he added that he 'was going to do this anyway'. The clinician did not persevere with introducing self-reward at the time; Darryl was generally not very compliant with his diary and the other tasks. However, the clinician continued to congratulate Darryl for completing the task and kept reminding him of the importance of rewarding himself, even if this was not actually part of the practice of that session.

Towards the end of the treatment, he asked Darryl to compare his mood with the way he was feeling at the time of the referral, Darryl spontaneously said: 'I have been treating myself a lot recently'. Although he had not actually completed the practice at the time, Darryl had understood the principle of rewarding himself; it took him longer than anticipated to be able to use it in everyday practice.

> The young person is encouraged to reward themselves for completing tasks.

Continuing activity scheduling throughout therapy

Activity scheduling can be continued throughout therapy with more challenging tasks being scheduled as progress is made. It is often useful to begin each session with a review of activity scheduling with examination of ratings of pleasure and achievement and situations of self-reward. This is particularly useful for young people who have become very withdrawn and socially isolated and where there is a significant degree of social anxiety involved in re-integration with peers. It may be necessary to break down activities into steps and take one at a time. For young people who begin to re-engage with their previous routines it can be helpful to continue activity scheduling alongside the new tasks approached in the following sessions in order to maintain behavioural gains. Success in activity scheduling is often associated with a lifting in mood that will assist in tackling cognitive elements of therapy.

> Activity scheduling should be continued throughout therapy particularly for young people who have become very socially withdrawn.

Managing sleep problems

Difficulties with sleeping are very common in depression. In young people these can manifest themselves in several ways. Problems may be apparent from the initial assessment but it is not unusual for the extent of them to emerge during the daily monitoring involved in activity scheduling. It is often helpful to include a supportive parent or carer in tackling these problems. In some circumstances medication may be prescribed. Completing a sleep diary (see Materials and worksheets) is helpful in identifying the nature and extent of difficulties. A clinician's prompt sheet is included in the Materials and worksheets.

General strategies that can be helpful

- Avoidance of stimulants, including tea and coffee, for several hours before bedtime.
- Relaxation and wind down before going to bed, including avoiding stressful conversations.
- Setting up a bedtime routine such as getting ready for the next day (clothes, books, homework etc.)
- Have a milky drink, bubble bath etc. Take a drink of water to bed and go to the toilet.
- Be aware that the average person takes up to an hour to get to sleep and the hour starts again each time you get out of bed.
- Don't get stressed about not getting to sleep, 'sleep' will come to you.

Difficulties in settling to sleep

At bedtime:

- relaxation recording
- listening to radio or story.

It can be helpful to have emotionally neutral background sound to distract from ruminations. Some commercially available relaxation exercise recordings focus on mental imagery which can assist.

Following a period of sleep:

- avoid lying in bed ruminating when awake
- try reading for a short time
- get up and do something monotonous before going back to bed.

It is important to distract from ruminating or worrying about sleep loss.

Day–night reversal

Day–night reversal involves the young person staying up all night and going to sleep around dawn then sleeping most of the day. Commonly this has developed as a result of a young person watching television or playing on a computer for hours because of difficulty sleeping. If there are no clear daytime routines (for instance school attendance) difficulties in falling asleep may escalate. The consequences can be particularly handicapping of social contact with family or peers. Effective intervention starts with trying to establish a time in the morning to get up, usually with a clear agreement for parental support and specific encouraging consequences for doing so. It is important that the young person takes responsibility for getting up, for instance by setting an alarm clock. This can gradually be moved earlier and bedtime set earlier, using some of the sleep hygiene measures outlined above at bedtime. Detailed monitoring can be helpful. This is a difficult problem to tackle effectively and requires substantial motivation on the part of the young person if it is to be addressed directly. It is important to avoid creating conflict with parents and hence to discourage parents from actively waking the young person themselves unless specifically requested.

> Tackling sleep problems involves establishing routines and preventing rumination.
>
> Individualised plans can be established, with appropriate parental support.

Self-monitoring

Self-monitoring is widely used both in assessment and monitoring change. This section outlines the principles particularly considering the need to have this in place as the young person enters the cognitive stages of therapy with the consequent need to record thoughts. The introduction of self-monitoring emphasises the self-help, collaborative nature of treatment. The young person is invited to reflect on how they feel and think. There are two stages. First the young person has to note that the target behaviour or feeling has occurred and secondly to record that it has happened. Key aspects in using self-monitoring include the following.

- Explanation that subsequent sessions will focus on the diaries produced.
- Specific, clearly defined targets that are meaningful to the young person.
- Detailed discussion of how to record material with provision of diary sheets or note books.
- Recordings should be made as soon as possible after the event. Discuss the practical aspects of this with the young person.
- Many young people are self-conscious of their writing skills. Simple ratings or frequency counts may be used.
- Many young people worry about parents or others reading their diaries. Emphasise confidentiality rules and explain that the clinician will look at diaries at the start of each session.

As therapy progresses self-monitoring reflects the development of session topics. Following activity scheduling for most young people it is appropriate to introduce recording of thinking and thoughts.

Self-monitoring is introduced with a remark such as 'depressed young people usually only pay attention to negative things that happen and negative thoughts and feelings about themselves'. The words negative/positive were selected for the introduction of self-monitoring as this concept will be important for the subsequent description of cognitions. The self-monitoring task begins with an explanation that young people may have difficulty identifying thoughts. Sometimes it can help to ask what the young person was thinking before coming to the appointment. The clinician then labels these as 'automatic thoughts' or 'the things you say to yourself'.

The clinician gives some representative examples that demonstrate a possible association between a pleasant and an unpleasant event and concurrent mood and thoughts. It is preferable that the examples are general ones to start with in order to normalise the process and facilitate understanding before addressing personal negative thinking. Clinicians may need to emphasise again the difference between feelings and thoughts.

During this part of the session, the clinician may identify:

- negative thoughts about self and the future
- positive thoughts about self and the future
- only paying attention to the negative.

Detecting automatic thoughts

Once the young person understands the definition of a thought and the presence of positive and negative cognitions the idea of the 'thought detective' can be used. This can be introduced by such comments as 'our minds are rarely completely blank, thoughts both positive and negative are crossing them all of the time. We are going to start work on catching these thoughts and putting them down in writing. You are going to become a sort of detective catching all of the thoughts going through your mind, a thought detective'. Chapter 6 covers use of thought records in more detail.

Examples of pleasant events and concurrent mood and thoughts:

Last weekend, I decided to invite two friends back to my house. We spent a few hours chatting and listening to music back at my house:

- I was *feeling* excited and happy.
- I was *thinking* that perhaps I should try to see my friends more often in the future.

On Monday I had my school report:

- I *felt* very pleased with myself.
- I *thought* that, although many of my friends had an even better report, I had tried really hard.

Examples of unpleasant events and concurrent mood/thoughts:

Yesterday, I asked about my grandmother's cancer. I was told that she is still very poorly:

- I *felt* sad and was tearful for the rest of the day.
- I *thought* that I was missing her very much.

On Wednesday, I was bullied by some young people in the playground:

- I *felt* really miserable.
- I *thought* that perhaps I should stand up for myself if that happens again.

6

Cognitive techniques

Sessions on emotional recognition and self-monitoring have worked on establishing the difference between feelings and thoughts and introduced thought monitoring. Negative automatic thoughts have been linked with depressed mood. The following sessions build on this work and constitute the main cognitive elements of the programme. As has been emphasised, some young people will spend all the sessions working with cognitive behavioural techniques whereas younger and less mature adolescents may not have the cognitive maturity to engage with this work. For them, the social skills and problem-solving sessions may be most appropriate.

Working with thoughts and thinking

This stage of cognitive behaviour therapy (CBT) will require several sessions and will focus upon the following:

- eliciting and recording automatic thoughts
- problems in detecting automatic thoughts
- identification of beliefs and faulty cognitive styles
- problems in identifying beliefs and cognitive styles
- cognitive restructuring
- evaluation of negative automatic thoughts (NATs) and beliefs
- strategies for dealing with NATs, dysfunctional beliefs and cognitive distortions.

In the cognitive theory of depression, thoughts are the primary experiences that lead to mood and behavioural symptoms. Challenging negative automatic thoughts (NATs) and core beliefs and identifying irrational thought processes are key aspects of therapy. Work in earlier sessions will have led to the identification of negative cognitions.

The cognitive work takes place in the context of collaborative empiricism; the clinician working together with the young person using factual data to understand thoughts and behaviours that maintain depression. Guided discovery involves helping the young person recognise dysfunctional thoughts using their own experience. This process can be introduced to the young person through standard vignettes which can demonstrate the relationship between thinking, feeling and behaving.

The noise in the dark vignette

Therapist:	*The way young people think and understand things affects how they feel and behave. For example, say a boy was in bed at home and he heard a crash in another bedroom. If he thinks 'there is a burglar in the room.' How do you think he would feel?*
Young person:	*Very scared.*
Therapist:	*How might he behave?*
Young person:	*Lie very still in bed. Or try to shout to his mum and dad.*
Therapist:	*Okay, so the boy thought that a burglar made the noise and he felt anxious and scared. Now let's say he heard the same noise and thought 'the window's open and something has blown down'. How would he feel?*
Young person:	*Still a bit scared but mainly worried that something was broken or annoyed that it had woken him up or sad that he might have lost something precious.*
Therapist:	*And would his behaviour be different following these thoughts?*
Young person:	*He would go and see what had happened.*
Therapist:	*So, this example shows us that there are a number of ways in which you can interpret situations. The way you interpret situations, affects your feelings and behaviour.*

Eliciting and recording automatic thoughts

The young person and clinician will act together as 'scientific collaborators' who will 'investigate' the young person's thinking. The clinician elicits the young person's ideas about the nature of their problems and uses an introduction such as: 'The ways in which we think about things affects our mood. Young people who are depressed often have ways of thinking that mean that they tend to look on the bad side of things. We are going to work together to identify these thoughts and challenge them. This is similar to the work we did at the beginning. Do you remember?'

Direct questioning

The use of concrete and specific questions is the most straightforward technique for eliciting automatic thoughts. Children and adolescents will not be used to registering the thoughts that are continuously passing through their minds and at the beginning will need prompting and help. Questions such as 'What thoughts were going through your mind then?' provide a starting point and can link in with the emotional recognition exercise in which the young person gives examples of different emotional states that he or she has recently experienced. It is very helpful to use the young person's emotional state in the therapy session and at times of strong emotion, to pause and help the young person to tell you the thoughts that are going through their mind 'now'. Increasing awareness of automatic thinking is a skill which needs to be learnt and it may help young people who are struggling with it to explain that everyone finds it difficult to begin with but with practice, it becomes 'second nature'.

> *Example (direct questioning): The clinician questions Paul about an episode described in his moods, thoughts and actions diary.*
>
> *Therapist:* Thank you for filling in your diary of your feelings over the last week, I want us to look at some of those moods in a bit more detail. Yesterday lunch time you felt depressed and sad, can you remember what thoughts were going through your mind?
> *Paul:*   No, not really.
> *Therapist:* Where were you when you started to feel depressed?
> *Paul:*   I was on the school field.
> *Therapist:* Were you alone or with some friends?
> *Paul:*   I was standing on my own as my friends had gone off to play football.
> *Therapist:* Describe what happened from the time when the bell went for lunch break.
> *Paul:*   I felt OK as I went into lunch with Mark and I sat with him and his friends. Then I went to the toilet and came out onto the field. I couldn't see my friends anywhere and then I spotted them running over to the playing fields. I started to feel very depressed.
> *Therapist:* What thoughts were going through your head when you saw your friends running off without you?
> *Paul:*   They are running away from me. They don't like me. I will never have any friends. I'm just a misfit.
> *Therapist:* Well done for remembering those thoughts. How are they making you feel now?
> *Paul:*   I feel depressed thinking about what happened.
> *Therapist:* Tell me what happened next.
> *Paul:*   I joined in with some other lads and then the bell went for lessons.

Therapist: *Do you see the link between the thoughts going through your head and your mood in the playground?*
Paul: *Yes.*
Therapist: *We need to go on to think more about those thoughts and examine them a bit more closely . . .*

Example (use of emotion in the therapy session): Emma, a depressed 15-year-old girl with school refusal illustrates this technique.

Emma: *It's in the mornings that I feel really bad as I can't get up and my mum keeps shouting me and I can't face the day . . . (Emma becomes tearful)*
Therapist: *You have become very upset when talking about those feelings you have in the mornings, what thoughts are going through your head at this moment?*
Emma: *I'll never get better, I'll never be a normal teenager, I'll never be able to go to school and if I don't then I'll never get a job and have a future, I'm just a failure.*
Therapist: *Are those thoughts passing through your head a lot of the times when you feel depressed?*
Emma: *Yes, and more too.*
Therapist: *There are links between your thoughts and your moods and we need to work a bit on those thoughts. The first stage is to practise 'catching' them and recording them in your diary . . .*

Examples of direct questions to help identify automatic thoughts

- What was going through your mind before you started to feel this way?

- What was going through your mind when you felt low/depressed?

- What were you thinking about your future?

- What were you afraid would happen?

- What were you thinking that other people think about you?

- Did you think in pictures? Were there any memories that came into your mind when or before you felt low?

Video playback

Many young people have difficulty reconstructing their past experiences from direct questioning and this may begin to feel like an interrogation. This task involves imagining that their life is on a video that can be played back to the mood or experience which has occurred. The young person can then play it back 'as if it were happening now' and recall the experience in detail.

When they are fully engaged in the process the clinician can ask them about their emotions and thoughts.

Unpleasant/pleasant events

The clinician gives some examples of pleasant or unpleasant events that are realistic, achievable and within the young person's control. Pictures or cartoons demonstrating common predicaments may be useful for younger adolescents. The young person is asked to imagine the scenarios, even if they have not actually experienced them and to identify the thoughts that these events might generate.

Pleasant events: 'It is the weekend and you have invited a couple of friends around to your house.'

- Feelings: happy, cheerful, excited.
- Thoughts: I like my friends, perhaps I should try to see them more often.

Unpleasant events: 'You are bullied in the school playground.'

- Feelings: scared, depressed, lonely.
- Thoughts: I'm a failure, I have no friends, perhaps I should try to stick up for myself in the future.

Mental imagery

When eliciting automatic thoughts it may help to use visual imagery to re-create a situation. This is an extension of the video playback technique. With help from the clinician, the young person creates a mental image of the situation, including visual and other sensory experiences and feelings. When the image has been created, the young person can be helped to focus on their cognitions and to recount accompanying automatic thoughts.

Darren, a 12-year-old boy, has been depressed following the separation of his parents.

Therapist: *So, over the last week you felt sad when you went to the football match with your best friend. What thoughts were going through your mind?*

Darren: *I don't know, I was really looking forward to it as we went with my friend's dad and brother.*

Therapist: *Cast your mind back to last Saturday and let's focus on how the day was from the start. Tell me about the morning and what happened during the early part of the day.*

Darren: *When I got up I was really looking forward to going to football. I had my breakfast with my mum and then watched the TV. Paul and his brother called for me after lunch and I was really excited then. Their dad drove us to the football ground.*

Therapist: *I want you to cast your mind back to the time when you went into the ground and found your seats. It may help to close your eyes for a minute to help remember what you could see around you, what you could hear and how you were feeling. Describe the picture in your mind to me.*

Darren: *I was sitting on the end of a row with Paul next to me, then his brother, then his dad. There were loads of people and everyone was very excited waiting for the players to come onto the pitch. Suddenly, I started to feel very sad and lonely.*

Therapist: *Can you remember the thoughts that were going through your mind as you were sitting there waiting for the players to come onto the pitch?*

Darren: *I was remembering the last time I went to see a football match with my dad before he left home. I could see the day in my mind and it was really strong. I could see my dad and me going into the ground and sitting in our seats that were in a different place from last Saturday. It was really strong and I felt really sad.*

Therapist: *Can you remember what the pictures in your mind made you think?*

Darren: *I thought 'It's not fair that Paul and Steven have a dad and I don't' 'My dad doesn't love me anymore . . .'*

Therapist: *So, even though you were doing something that you really enjoy (watching football), you felt very sad. Can you see the connection between those thoughts about your dad and how you were feeling?*

Darren: *(nods)*

Therapist: *Those are the automatic thoughts that we have been talking about which are very important to 'catch' and to monitor. I expect those pictures and memories come into your mind from time to time too. It will be important for us to talk about them and to understand them better . . .*

Role play

Role play can be used to re-create a situation vividly so that the concurrent automatic thoughts become available. It can be used as an extension of imagery. The young person plays themselves and the clinician plays key individuals in the young person's life. Alternatively, reverse role play can be useful in which case the clinician plays the part of the young person, empathising with them and suggesting some possible thoughts which might have been influencing the young person's mood. In the following example, Emma had noticed that she felt depressed whenever she spent any time with her cousin of the same age. The role play helped the young person to verbalise her automatic thoughts triggered by contact with her cousin.

Example (role play):

Therapist: *(As the cousin) Hi Emma, how are you? Do you want to come out with us at the weekend?*

Emma: *OK. Where are you going?*

Therapist: *To the pictures with Danny and Michelle.*

Emma: *I'll have to ask my mum . . . (Emma looks sad)*

Therapist: *What are the thoughts that are running through your mind now?*

Emma: *Laura's got loads of friends, her mum lets her do what she wants, she only asks me because she feels sorry for me.*

Therapist: *How do those thoughts make you feel?*

Emma: *They make me feel sad and guilty because everyone else thinks Laura's fantastic and she just makes me feel useless.*

Techniques using written materials

Questionnaires

Younger adolescents find verbalising their thoughts difficult and it is often helpful to use written techniques to facilitate their communication. During the assessment, questionnaires may have been used to explore symptoms of depression. For example, the Moods and Feelings Questionnaire (Costello and Angold, 1988) is a 33-item questionnaire with questions based on Diagnostic and Statistical Manual of Mental Disorder (DSM) criteria for depression. The young person is required to respond 'true', 'sometimes true' or 'not true' to statements such as 'I thought there was nothing good for me in the future', and 'I thought bad things would happen to me'. It can be useful to go through responses and use them as a focus for eliciting negative thoughts.

More specific questionnaires aimed at identifying negative thinking (for example, Cognitive Triad Inventory – Child (Kaslow *et al.*, 1992) and Automatic Thoughts Questionnaire (Stark *et al.*, 1990) (see Chapter 3) can also provide material for discussion.

Young people who like writing can be invited as a homework task to write about 'Myself as others see me', a description of themselves in the third person. This can be a helpful method of eliciting negative automatic thoughts about self as well as being of benefit in exploring maladaptive styles of thinking and beliefs.

Sentence completion tasks may also be useful, particularly for younger adolescents. These can be designed with a particular young person in mind. The young person is asked to complete sentences about themselves, their lives and their views which again can be a focus for eliciting negative thoughts and then exploring the context and triggers for them. Typical sentences would be: 'My biggest worry is . . .'; 'People don't like me because . . .'; 'I hope to become . . .'

Emotional pie chart

This visual technique involves construction of a pie chart of the emotions that the young person has experienced during a particular day. Each area of the chart represents a feeling such as 'worry', 'anger', 'sadness' or 'happiness'. This can help to put intense short-lived emotions in context and, as a continuation of the emotional recognition exercise, provide a focus for questioning about automatic thoughts.

> *Carl, age 13, described in his diary a low mood following an argument with his older sister that led to an argument between their parents. He became stuck when asked how he had felt.*
>
> Therapist: *I wonder if you had several different feelings. What feelings can you remember at the time?*
> Carl: *I was worried about my Mum. Sad and angry. Guilty as well.*
> Therapist: *Let's look at that on a pie chart (draws large circle). If we think of the whole pie as 100% of your feelings at the time, about how much was angry? Can you draw the lines in the right place?*
> Carl: *About 50% I think. I thought that my sister hates me and is always getting me into trouble.*
> Therapist: *Let's make a note of those thoughts as well. What about sad feelings?*
> Carl: *Well about 25%. I thought that my parents might split up again.*
> Therapist: *What about feeling worried?*
> Carl: *I think about 10% worrying that they might split up.*
> Therapist: *You said you felt guilty too. Were there any other feelings?*
> Carl: *No. I thought it was all my fault.*

Emotionally meaningful material

The young person can be invited to bring to the session examples of song lyrics or poems that they have found personally meaningful. These can be used as a basis for exploring situations from their own experience with associated feelings and thoughts.

A variety of techniques can be used to help young people identify negative automatic thoughts including:

- direct questioning
- video playback/as if
- unpleasant/pleasant events
- mental imagery

- role play
- written materials.

A clinician prompt sheet on eliciting and recording NATs is included in the Materials and worksheets.

Techniques for recording automatic thoughts

Detection and monitoring

At the beginning of therapy, the young person is learning to detect automatic thoughts and monitor their mood states. The therapist may start with a simple exercise involving counting thoughts as they occur. The young person can be encouraged to carry their diary with them and record thoughts by using ticks or other simple entries.

Diaries

Methods for recording thoughts, activities and feelings have been introduced over the course of the treatment programme. The diary is an important part of the treatment. Several examples are included in the Materials and worksheets.

Thought charts

The young person can be asked to keep a thought chart which has three columns: 1. event; 2. feelings; 3. thoughts. An example is given in the Materials and worksheets. The young person is asked to monitor their feelings closely. When they have a strong feeling or reaction to something, they should concentrate on using the following questions, together with any techniques they have learnt from the sessions, and record their thoughts on their chart.

- What was going through my mind just before I started to feel this way?
- What am I afraid might happen?
- What does this mean about how the other person(s) feel(s)/think(s) about me?
- What images or memories do I have in this situation?

Completion of the chart is first demonstrated with examples in the session.

'Hot' thoughts

Once the young person has grasped the concepts of automatic thinking and self-monitoring, they will quickly build up long lists of automatic thoughts and it is necessary to help them to 'sift' through this material and identify the crucial thought or thoughts which are influencing their mood, their 'hot' thoughts. These will represent the important areas of negativity that it will be crucial to address in working with the young person on their experience of depression.

Review of daily diary

Therapy sessions will be oriented around the young person's diary recordings. The quality and quantity of recording will provide helpful information for the clinician and will enable a decision to be made regarding moving on to challenging negative thoughts.

> Diaries and thought charts can be used to record automatic thoughts.

Problems in detecting automatic thoughts

The following are specific problems that may occur when undertaking cognitive work with young people. A broader discussion of possible problems in therapy is addressed in Chapter 11.

Lack of specific negative automatic thoughts

For some, the emotional recognition exercises fail to reveal any relationship between situations, moods and thoughts. The young person consistently describes pervasive, generalised non-specific depressive thinking. In this case it may be helpful to proceed to exploring and eliciting beliefs as described in the next section, rather than focusing on situationally driven NATs.

Young people with learning difficulties

The assessment process will have outlined the emotional and cognitive abilities of the young person and techniques used in therapy need to be modified accordingly. Young people need to be able to read and write to participate in CBT unless there is major modification of the programme. Younger, less able adolescents will benefit more from behavioural techniques including activity scheduling and social problem-solving exercises. It can be very helpful to involve the family in checking out differing views of problems and situations with a view to identifying distortions in the young person's thinking. Concrete examples and the use of modelling by the clinician can often be helpful. Techniques will need to be simplified and broken down into smaller steps with regular checking that concepts have been understood.

Not completing the mood diary

Early in therapy the young person may keep an unstructured diary of events and occurrences in preference to the mood diary. Usually, the volume of recorded material is directly proportional to the pervasiveness of the depressed mood. Sometimes the diary has been completed in retrospect just before the session. It is important that the young person understands the importance of home practice. Plenty of time needs to be reserved towards the end of the session for the setting of the task and including the clinician and young person working through an example. It may be useful to have an exploration with the young person of their anticipated problems in keeping the diary and how to overcome them. Much time and attention needs to be given to using the diary in the following session as a practical demonstration of the importance of home practice. In addition, exploring the adolescent's cognitions regarding the task can be revealing. It may be that the homework was regarded as 'a waste of time' and related to a generalised hopelessness about the future and the potential for recovery. It may be that the adolescent started the task but did not complete it because of thoughts of incompetence and fears of what the clinician might think. It may be that not completing the task reflected a tendency to procrastinate, perfectionist tendencies or generalised lack of motivation and inactivity. These can all be used as a focus for therapeutic work within the session. If the young person simply forgot to bring the diary, their recall of its contents can be discussed.

Feeling 'overwhelmed' with negative automatic thoughts

Sometimes, raising awareness of automatic thoughts and encouraging recording them can lead to a deterioration in mood and a feeling of being 'overwhelmed' by hopelessness. It may be helpful to outline this as a potential problem both to the young person and to their parent or carer at the outset and to reassure them that the next stage in treatment involves teaching skills for dealing with this eventuality. Activity scheduling, simple measures for sleep problems and checking strategies for dealing with powerful emotions can increase the adolescent's perceived control. The clinician can also encourage the rationale that by writing down the thoughts it may be possible to temporarily disarm them.

Identification of beliefs and thinking errors

Three levels of thoughts are addressed in cognitive therapy: automatic thoughts, underlying assumptions and schemas. Automatic thoughts are the immediate unplanned thoughts (words, memories and images) that flow through our minds throughout the day. Underlying assumptions are the beliefs and rules that guide our lives. They include 'should' statements ('a daughter should love her mother') and conditional 'if . . . then' statements ('if people get to know me then they will reject me'). Underlying assumptions guide behaviour although they are not articulated consciously. Schemas have been described as screens or filters that process and code stimuli. They are absolute core beliefs about the self, the world and others. The three levels of thought are interconnected. At the deepest level core beliefs such as 'I'm unlovable' give rise to assumptions such as 'when people get to know me they won't like me' and automatic thoughts such as 'nobody will speak to me at the party'. In CBT with adolescents there is less differential between the layers of thinking and work with schemas and assumptions may go alongside work with automatic thoughts. The following are techniques for eliciting the deeper more enduring thought patterns of young people.

Rationale

The working model for describing automatic thoughts to young people is useful in presenting a rationale for working at a deeper level. Using the self-monitoring diary and examples from therapy sessions, an experience can be divided into emotional or mood components, thoughts, behaviours and physical reactions. The work on automatic thoughts should be reviewed and the scene or agenda set for probing more deeply to understand the origin of these with a view to making changes to thinking.

Greenberger and Padesky (1995) make a very useful analogy. They describe automatic thoughts as being similar to flowers and weeds in a garden. The weeds can be cut making more room for the flowers to grow. Techniques for cutting weeds are likened to dealing with negative automatic thoughts in cognitive therapy. Sometimes even if you keep cutting weeds they grow back and suffocate the flowers. In order to deal with them more permanently, deeper changes involving the roots of the weeds are needed. This work in cognitive therapy concerns the deeper thinking patterns and the rules by which we live our lives.

Techniques for identifying dysfunctional beliefs:

- Socratic questionning
- offering hypotheses
- family interviewing.

Identifying dysfunctional beliefs involves a process of guided discovery that the clinician and young person embark upon together. The clinician asks a series of questions intended to lead the young person to examine their beliefs and behaviours and by so doing weaken their belief in them. Questions are not primarily used to gather information, but to guide self-discovery. This collaborative style of therapeutic communication will be liberating for some young people. However, engagement requires a level of insight and creative or lateral thinking that will not be available to some who may find it threatening or intimidating.

Techniques of Socratic questioning, the downward arrow technique, innocent questioning and reflective empathy are described below.

Socratic questioning

Socratic questioning involves the use of a logical series of questions that should lead the adolescent to challenge beliefs or thoughts. Questions are used not only to obtain information but also to raise issues and to offer suggestions. The clinician must be careful not to appear as if persecuting or cross-examining the young person.

> *A depressed 16-year-old girl was convinced that she was useless at her schoolwork. Rather than stating that her thinking was wrong, the clinician asked her 'Can you help me to understand how your teachers can tell you that you are a very good pupil, you get high grades in your recent examination, but somehow you think that you are nearly useless at schoolwork? Does that all fit together?'*
> *(asked in a puzzled manner).*

Socratic questioning sometimes evokes responses such as 'I don't know'. In such circumstances the question may be either repeated using different words, or if there is an obvious misunderstanding the clinician can repeat the question with statements such as 'I don't seem to have asked that question very well. I'll try and put it differently . . .' or try a different approach.

Downward arrow technique

This refers to a series of questions addressing the emotional significance of a specific event. The intention is to take the interpretation of the event to a progressively deeper level guiding the young person to understand the beliefs and assumptions that led them to experience or interpret the particular event in the way that they did. In essence, the clinician repeatedly asks 'why?' or 'so what?' as a probe. 'What would it mean to you if. . . .' is often the easiest and least provocative way of framing questions. It is particularly useful to apply to negative automatic thoughts and helps the young person to identify the underlying beliefs from which they arise.

The first example using the downward arrow technique is with Aaron, a 15-year-old boy who is worrying about his forthcoming exams:

Aaron: *I feel sure I am going to fail, I spend all my time worrying about the work I am not doing and can't concentrate on the work I am trying to do.*

Therapist: So while you are trying to study, tell me about some of the thoughts that are running through your mind.

Aaron: When I am studying for maths I am thinking, 'I am going to fail' 'I won't be able to answer a single question'.

Therapist: So if you failed the maths exam, why would that be so upsetting to you?

Aaron: Everyone would know I am a failure.

Therapist: So, if you failed and people knew about that, why would that be so upsetting?

Aaron: I would feel terrible and embarrassed and like a complete failure.

Therapist: So, why do you think it means so much to you what other people think?

Aaron: (pause) . . . I think I need people's approval to feel happy and worthwhile. . . .

It was then possible for the clinician to work through examples of thinking errors and distortions to challenge with the young person their need to please others.

The following example is with Sarah, age 16 years, describing a depressed mood that occurred in the previous week in the context of an argument with her mother.

Therapist: You felt very low and angry after your mum had shouted at you. You listed some of the NATs that were triggered. Which do you think was the 'hot' thought?

Sarah: The thoughts are usually the same. 'I'm hopeless, everything I do is wrong, she is never pleased with me, she doesn't love me . . .' The thought that really makes me unhappy is the last one and it is making me unhappy now even thinking about it.

Therapist: Of course it is upsetting for anyone to think that their mum doesn't love them but it does seem to come into your head quite frequently and despite what your mum says. It seems to be an idea that you hold about yourself and maybe the next step is to examine this more closely. . . .

Innocent questioning

The clinician takes a confused stance, asking for more clarification in order to probe the young person's thoughts and beliefs. For example, Lucy appeared to the clinician to have the belief that she is inferior and never as good as others. Socratic questioning is used to enable her to understand this belief and start to question it.

Lucy: There is no point in my going to the party, I haven't got anything to wear and no one will talk to me . . .

Therapist: Maybe you can help me understand how so many people have

described you as capable, kind and sociable, but you think you're
worthless. . . . I really feel puzzled by that . . .

Reflective empathy

Young people often expect there to be a right or wrong answer to a question
and will try to produce this for the clinician. They will be unfamiliar with the
style of Socratic questioning and will require time and patience to respond.
They are also very sensitive to tone of voice and may quickly close down if
they detect any sense of disbelief or parental side-taking on the part of the
clinician. It is very important not to seem to ridicule or devalue young
person's thoughts and beliefs and to be mindful of personality characteristics, religious and moral beliefs.

For example, Lewis, a 15-year-old boy was very unhappy after his best
friend left school fairly suddenly during the summer holidays.

Therapist:	*Describe some of the thoughts that were going through your mind when you felt very low and unhappy in school on Tuesday.*
Lewis:	*I have no friends, Why didn't he tell me he was leaving, I shall probably never see him again.*
Therapist:	*OK, so he left without telling you, why would that be so upsetting to you?*
Lewis:	*Why do you think? We've been friends for 4 years, how would you feel?*
Therapist:	*He didn't actually tell you he was leaving and you think that you will never see him again . . .*
Lewis:	*It means that the friendship was nothing to him. He didn't feel the same way . . .*
Therapist:	*You think that he didn't feel the same way . . .*
Lewis:	*I thought he did at the time . . .*
Therapist:	*If your thoughts that he didn't feel the same way were true then why would that be so upsetting for you?*
Lewis:	*It would mean that I had trusted him and he had let me down, that I had made a fool of myself . . .*

This gentle approach continued and enabled Lewis to talk about
uncertainties about his sexuality and difficulties in trusting. These were emo-
tive issues. By taking a more straightforward downward arrow technique the
clinician could come across as too challenging.

Offering hypotheses

The clinician may have developed a cognitive formulation of the young
person's underlying beliefs and assumptions and it is helpful to spend time
working on the formulation with the young person. The clinician may take a

leading role, hypothesising thoughts and beliefs for the young person in ways that may help the young person to elicit their dysfunctional beliefs and attitudes. Suggestions may be accepted as stated or revised to more accurately reflect the actual belief.

In the following example, Darren, a 12-year-old very bright boy, is talking about his distress at his parents' separation.

Darren: *I never see my dad now and I know my mum is unhappy all of the time. I wish he hadn't left . . .*

Therapist: *When you feel sad, how do your thoughts go?*

Darren: *I feel angry with that woman for taking him away . . .*

Therapist: *Do you remember how you listed out lots of thoughts you have about your dad, your mum and you and what was going on for you in school around the time your dad left? Those thoughts often seem to come from deep in your head and I am wondering if deep down you blame yourself for your dad leaving*

Darren: *(tearful) He was only ever bothered about my school marks. He was really cross with me for not coming top in maths.*

Therapist: *Do you think that your maths mark was involved in your dad leaving your mum?*

Darren: *Put like that I suppose it sounds stupid but I do blame myself for not being good enough for him as a son and also for causing arguments between mum and dad.*

> Use of questioning to elicit beliefs:
>
> * look for themes in thought records
>
> * core beliefs concern oneself, others, the world
>
> * take young person's descriptions to a deeper level by asking 'if that were true what would it mean to you?' (downward arrow technique)
>
> * re-frame statements to challenge the young person's beliefs. For example 'Can you explain how you consistently get top marks for your exams but believe that you are a failure at school?'
>
> * ask for more clarification 'I'm puzzled that you think that you are disliked yet you went out with friends three times last week?'

Family interviewing

The techniques above can be used in sessions one to one with the young person. When working with adolescents it is commonly the case that discrepancies between beliefs of family members are important in maintaining depressive disorders. This is usually discovered in the course of individual work and it can be very helpful to attempt to identify beliefs of parents and the young person in a joint session. Usually, it becomes clear over the course of individual cognitive therapy that the young person is not responding and greater parental involvement is indicated. The young person should be involved in planning this and it is often helpful to complete each session by inviting the parent to join for some feedback. It may be useful to hold a family session aiming at eliciting beliefs of individual family members and sharing a cognitive formulation with the family. The techniques for eliciting beliefs and assumptions can be used in a family session as illustrated by the following example.

> *Sarah is a 15-year-old girl who took an overdose of paracetamol follow-ing an argument with her mother. Sarah had never known her natural father. Her mum had a succession of boyfriends all of whom Sarah had disliked. Her mother was on her own at the time of the overdose and herself quite depressed. Sarah had also just split up with her boyfriend and had many symptoms of depression. She had been attending for individual sessions and had been coming alone. Sarah and the clinician planned a family session to review Sarah's progress. The following is part of a session with Sarah and her mother.*

Therapist: Thank you for coming. The purpose of our meeting is to review Sarah's progress and give you some feedback.

Mother: I haven't seen much improvement in Sarah's attitude and we keep on arguing but she has been going out with her friends more and hasn't looked so upset. I keep thinking she is going to take another overdose.

Therapist: It must have been a shock to you when Sarah took the over-dose and we talked about it at the time. If she took another one what would that mean to you?

Mother: I'd failed as a mother.

Therapist: To fail as a mother is upsetting, is that something you worry about a lot?

Mother: I always wanted to make up for my mother who was never there for me and didn't give a damn and I feel I've been a worse mother to Sarah despite trying not to.

Therapist: How do you feel about what your mum has just said, Sarah?

Sarah: I am surprised that she thinks that as I always think it's me that's failed her. She never talks about my gran and I never know what happened, just that she had me at 16 and left home. I blame me being born for wrecking her life.

Therapist: It is striking to me that these are important misunderstand-ings. Sarah believes that she is not trustworthy and unable to please you (to mum) and your mum, Sarah, believes that she has failed you as a mother . . .

Identification of thinking errors

Faulty cognitive styles or cognitive distortions are habitual ways of interpreting information that alter reality such that an unnecessarily negative view of the self, future and world is generated. The term 'thinking errors' is preferred in working with adolescents. A handout listing thinking errors with examples can be useful in clinical practice and this is included in the Materials and worksheets. It is not necessary for the clinician to be preoccupied with classification but examples of logical errors and their nature can be helpful in explanation. The following categories are not logically mutually exclusive. The use of humour in giving examples of thinking error can aid insight and lifting of mood.

All or nothing thinking

'All or nothing thinking' is the tendency to see things in extremes. This is common in adolescence and experiences are frequently either 'brilliant' or 'disastrous'. Emotions are in terms of love or hate and friends are either very close or enemies.

> *Emily, a 14-year-old girl, described meeting a new friend at the youth club. She later described her to her mother: 'She's brilliant! She looks really cool, she has loads of friends and a boyfriend, she's really clever and she's got a brilliant mum. She's asked me to go on holiday with her and be her best mate!' The next week, Emily's new friend was talking to another girl and did not smile when Emily caught her eye. Emily described this to her mother in floods of tears: 'She hates me. She doesn't want to hang around with me any more, I'll never have any friends, I'm useless . . .'*

Clues to all or nothing thinking are the use of extreme adjectives such as 'totally . . .', 'absolutely . . .', 'brilliant', 'disastrous' etc.

Overgeneralisation

This refers to the tendency to use one specific example to draw general conclusions. Just because one experience has been unsuccessful, it does not mean that life in general is unsuccessful.

> *Brian aged 15 described not being picked for the football team. 'I wasn't picked to play on Saturday, I'm completely useless, I may as well give up football. The manager thinks I am rubbish!' Despite playing regularly for the team, when he was not picked for one match Brian extrapolated from this that he is useless as a person and hopeless at football. He overgeneralised a decision made about his footballing skills to include himself.*

Mental filter

This refers to the tendency to dwell on the negatives and ignore the positives, looking at the world through 'dark glasses'. This dysfunctional style involves young people taking the most gloomy view of themselves and their situation. Despite information to the contrary they may persist in blocking out any rays of sunshine and hold on doggedly to their negative views.

> *Jill aged 16 was invited to a friend's party. Many of her friends were there and complimented her on her outfit. She appeared to be really enjoying herself. Towards the end of the evening, she was talking with her friend who mentioned that a boy Jill liked had been at the party but had left early. He had not spoken to Jill. Over the rest of the evening, Jill became gloomy and pre-occupied and when her sister asked her the next day whether she had had a good time, she snapped angrily that it had been awful and she had been snubbed by a boy. Jill had completely disregarded the compliments and enjoyment of earlier in the evening and focused on one small aspect, her interpretation of which had spoilt the whole experience.*

Discounting the positives

This refers to the tendency to turn something positive into something negative. In this way the 'victim' both misses out on the positive and secondly experiences a negative experience.

> *Jane was recovering from anorexia nervosa. She had slowly gained weight but had found this very difficult and experienced severe and persistent cognitive distortions. A relative came to visit her family who had not seen Jane since she had been ill in hospital. She was delighted to see Jane who had obviously made progress and said 'Jane you look really well!' Jane was furious and interpreted this to mean 'You look like you have put on weight'. She had turned a genuine compliment into further evidence that she is fat, ugly and unacceptable.*

Jumping to conclusions (mind reading and fortune telling)

Young people who are depressed frequently predict the future without sufficient evidence. Negative thoughts about the future are used as evidence for negative outcomes leading to pervasive avoidance. This 'fortune telling' is very common.

> *Jenny suffered from very low moods and a chaotic eating pattern. She complained incessantly that she had no friends and was ugly, fat and hated by everybody. When any suggestions were made by her mother or her clinician for ways of meeting friends she would refuse saying 'There's no point, nobody will speak to me and I'll feel even worse!'*

Jenny had predicted a negative outcome without any evidence that this was likely.

The second form of jumping to conclusions is the tendency to 'mind read'. This refers to the mistaken assumption that you can predict what other people are or will think. Again this is a common cognitive distortion and involves predicting the future with insufficient evidence.

Emma has been avoiding drama lessons since she was given a border-line mark for her last assignment. Her teacher appreciated that she had missed some of the work due to illness and thought very highly of Emma's abilities. She had tried to arrange an appointment with Emma to discuss the mark. Emma had avoided the meeting and explained her thoughts to her clinician: 'She (the teacher) thinks I'm stupid. I've really blown it now. She wants me to leave the class and won't let me sit the exam. She just wants to humiliate me in front of my mum and friends.' It is clear that Emma is predicting the content of the meeting with her teacher and her teacher's views of her on the basis of no real evidence and that these thoughts are leading to avoidance.

Magnification or minimisation

This involves blowing things up completely out of proportion or shrinking their importance inappropriately. Like the 'dark glasses' analogy (mental filter, see p. 99), young people understand this form of cognitive distortion to be likened to looking at the world through binoculars. If you look through the correct lenses, the image is enlarged, if you look through the reverse way, everything is shrunken.

Emotional reasoning

This is where a young person makes a judgement about themselves, the world or the future based on the experience of an emotion, for example, guilt is a common emotion experienced in depression. A young person feels guilty and therefore takes the experience of that to mean that they must have done something wrong. Hopelessness is also common. The clinician's task is to help the young person see that experiencing an emotion does not mean that the assumed cause is a fact.

'Should' statements

Should statements are often maladaptive and by pursuing these statements the clinician may uncover negative emotions and behaviours. For example 'I should be able to understand my homework'. These statements show unhappiness with a given situation but do not help in problem-solving.

Labelling

Labelling is where one particular characteristic or event then becomes the definition of that person or event. For example a girl who cried on one occasion when she fell over becomes a 'softie'. A young person may label themselves in a harsh manner and therefore have a negative bias.

Personalisation and blame

Personalisation is where a person interprets an event as an indication about themselves. For example in a social situation that goes badly on one occasion the young person may decide that they will never be able to make new friends.

Common thinking errors (examples and challenges) are:

- all or nothing thinking (find a middle way)

- over-generalisation (judge everything on its own merits)

- discounting the positives (turning a compliment into an insult)

- jumping to conclusions (mind reading, fortune telling)

- magnification/minimisation (looking at the world through binoculars)

- emotional reasoning (because you feel guilty you think that you have done something wrong)

- should statements (beating yourself up)

- labelling (one swallow doesn't make a summer)

- personalisation (taking things personally).

Problems in identifying beliefs and cognitive styles

Some problems with detecting automatic thoughts have been discussed earlier. The following problems can be seen as a continuation of the previous discussion and relate to the techniques described in this section.

Difficulties in differentiating beliefs from thoughts

It is helpful to use metaphorical explanations such as the one described with weeds (NATs) and their roots (beliefs). In practice it will not always be necessary or helpful to make the distinction. There will be some young people who will benefit from a cognitive approach who will not be able to use a detailed cognitive formulation that incorporates dysfunctional assumptions and how these arose. It is difficult for a novice clinician to use these techniques and as such it is helpful to discuss in supervision how to apply them and to have opportunities to listen to more experienced clinicians using them. A visual diagram of the cognitive formulation outlining the levels of cognitive functioning can also be used to illustrate the distinction.

Young people's need for approval

As a clinician it is important to be led by the young person and to facilitate the young person in gaining an understanding of their depression and how it has arisen. Young people seek approval and it can cause difficulties when compliance with home practice and working within the session is influenced by a need for the clinician's approval. The clinician will need to be reticent in giving formulations that have not been initiated by the young person. This may be a particular challenge in working with young people with learning difficulties.

Negative life situations

Frequently adolescents in therapy describe mood disorders that are occurring in the context of multiple problems at home and in relationships. These may include experiences of physical, emotional and sexual abuse, fear of violence and crime and emotional deprivation. The beliefs elicited in the context of therapy may be accurate for example, being let down by adults or friends. It will often be possible to work with identifying cognitive styles and dysfunctional cognitive processing, however, it must be recognised that negative cognitions related to mood disorders may be accurate, in which case cognitive restructuring techniques are not appropriate. Other problem-solving and coping skills should be used and these are described in Chapter 7. The young person may respond with sarcasm or anger when their beliefs and thinking styles are explored. The way forward is to review the problem list and therapeutic goals to identify realistic areas for change.

Family involvement

The techniques discussed in the previous section are used primarily with the young person alone. It is difficult for the clinician to get a sense of how much or little progress is being made without regular feedback. Parents may feel excluded by the individual time that the young person is receiving and need information. General issues of parental involvement are discussed in Chapter 9. With respect to eliciting assumptions and beliefs, it will be helpful to consider the need for parental involvement both to facilitate this work and to support the adolescent with it. When engaged in detecting thoughts and beliefs, adolescents will often feel initially worse and overwhelmed with their situations. Parental or carer support will be helpful here. Also, young people may find that they can understand the model and use it but do not feel any better. Sharing beliefs and thoughts with parents, subject to the young person's agreement, can help in starting to evaluate them and in determining the distorted cognitions and thinking errors that can then form a focus of intervention.

Cognitive restructuring

The next stage in therapy is cognitive restructuring. The aim of cognitive restructuring is to challenge negative thinking and teach young people more adaptive thought patterns. They are helped to recognise the negative impact of their thought processes and to replace dysfunctional cognitions with more accurate and adaptive thought patterns. The target symptoms of cognitive restructuring are automatic thoughts, negative self-statements, interpretations, beliefs, and cognitive distortions. The sessions follow a format of discussion of material brought to sessions on thought records with appropriate discussion and challenge using the techniques described below. A clinician prompt sheet is included in the Materials and worksheets.

> Cognitive restructuring involves learning ways of observing and monitoring thoughts, evaluating them and seeking evidence about whether they are appropriate.
>
> Using the thought diary the clinician introduces strategies for helping the young person challenge negative thoughts and thinking styles. This takes place over several sessions.

Evaluation of negative automatic thoughts and beliefs

Having identified the actual situation or event that is upsetting or significant in triggering the depressed mood, the thoughts and beliefs should be examined for evidence of thinking errors. When exploration and evaluation has revealed negative cognitions, the goal of the clinician is then to encourage cognitive change. The clinician's style continues to be one of collaborative empiricism, helping the young person learn about their thoughts and thinking style and appraise events and feelings realistically.

Reality testing

This involves examining the evidence for a thought or belief. Although depressed people characteristically view their world in a negative light, the clinician should not fall into a trap of assuming that all of the young person's negative thoughts or statements are invalid. The clinician and young person examine a sample of the young person's thoughts in collaboration. The basis or evidence for each thought should be subjected to the scrutiny of reality testing. Ratings of how much the young person believes a negative statement then re-rating after challenging can be helpful.

Angelica, age 15, expresses the belief that no one would ever like her:

Therapist:　*Why do you feel that no one would like you?*
Angelica:　*Because I'm ugly.*
Therapist:　*Didn't you tell me that a boy came up to you at the weekend to talk to you and said you were pretty and he fancied you?*
Angelica:　*Yes, but he didn't mean it.*
Therapist:　*Why do you think he didn't mean it?*
Angelica:　*I don't know . . . because I'm ugly.*
Therapist:　*Isn't it possible that he said it because he meant it?*
Angelica:　*I guess . . . I don't know.*
Therapist:　*Can you think of any other reason for him to say it, then?*
Angelica:　*No.*
Therapist:　*Isn't it likely, then, that he was telling the truth?*
Angelica:　*I guess.*
Therapist:　*So, isn't it likely that he did like you and did think you were pretty?*
Angelica:　*I guess.*
Therapist:　*So, is it incorrect that people don't like you because you are so ugly?*
Angelica:　*I guess so.*

The essence of reality testing is to enable the person to correct distortions. An analysis of meaning and attitudes expresses the unreasonableness and self-defeating nature of the attitudes. The clinician does not accept the young person's conclusions and inferences at face value but pursues them to determine their validity.

Once the young person is familiar with self-monitoring skills they will recognise that certain cognitions are particularly frequent at times when feeling depressed. Cognitions often reflect a person's belief in their lack of competency, unattractiveness or social isolation. The clinician helps the young person to recognise these negative biases in their choice of interpretations and how they tend to make negative inferences even in the face of contradictory evidence.

Young people do not change their views simply because they become aware of their biased interpretations. The accuracy of each interpretation requires a careful examination so that the young person can improve both observational, self-monitoring skills and the ability to form realistic and logical inferences so that they can challenge their thinking themselves.

Reality testing

- Rate believability (out of 100%). For instance '*I have no friends. 80%*'.

- Examine evidence in favour of belief and write one sentence that summarises this. For instance '*I used to enjoy going out with my friends but since my best friend got a boyfriend, another friend moved away and my sister changed schools I don't go out much.*'

- Examine evidence not in support of the thought or belief. For instance, '*My friend still phones me a lot and asks me out. I'm planning to go to stay with my other friend soon.*'

- If someone I know was in the situation what would I say to them?

- Create a balanced thought or belief. For instance '*At the moment my friendship group has changed. Various things have happened at once. My friends still care for me but I need to make new friends now.*'

Use of behavioural experiments

Behavioural experiments are designed to test the reliability of a young person's beliefs or predictions. The clinician and young person identify the experiment, predict what will happen, put it to the test as a homework task, note the results and then re-assess the original presumption or belief on which the experiment was based. It is a useful approach in operationalising beliefs, particularly for young people who have difficulty with reasoning in the abstract.

> *Lewis, age 15, believed that following some absences from practice sessions, he would not be able to get back into his local football team. This was his justification for not attending them. In the session he decided to telephone the coach who organised the team to talk about getting back on form and whether it was possible to attend training sessions for the rest of the season. The coach advised him that he would meet him at the next session and that they could devise a training programme to get his fitness back. This was a successful experiment for Lewis in challenging the belief that he was hopeless at football since losing his fitness and would never be any good.*

Behavioural experiments can be useful in challenging beliefs:

- operationalise beliefs, implications if the belief were true
- design a simple experiment to test and record what happens as home practice.

Challenging all or nothing thinking

All or nothing thinking is common in depressed adults, and is often evident in the thinking of normal adolescents. Thus, normal adolescents may be 'completely down' one week and 'really happy' the next. The key principle is to encourage the young person to work with the clinician to develop more graded emotional and cognitive responses to the world.

Rating thoughts or feelings on a scale: for example, the young person might be asked to rate on a 1 to 10 scale of depressed mood 'what was the rating when your father failed to visit you that weekend?' or 'how much did you believe that it was your fault that your father did not come?'. The emotions or belief in thoughts can be re-rated following discussion and thought challenges. The young person can then see a change in ratings in a positive direction, but not to the other extreme.

Adopting a proportional standpoint: alternatively, the young person could be asked, 'how much of your depression today is a result of your father not coming at the weekend?'. Using an emotional pie chart (see p. 88) may assist in demonstrating mixed feelings. Alternatively, if the young person is blaming him or herself for father's non-attendance ('it is all my fault that he did not come because I was nasty to him last time'), the clinician can challenge this assumption with questions such as 'what proportion of responsibility for your dad not coming was yours?' This can start with generating as many ideas as possible about why the meeting did not occur. The young person can then re-rate beliefs after they have been tested.

> All or nothing thinking is common in young people.
>
> • Rating scales can be used to assess believability.
> • Challenge evidence and adopt the middle ground.

Reframing and relabelling

This involves exploring the meaning of a particular belief and identifying a positive rather than negative approach to it.

> Lufti age 16 hoped to visit Pakistan with her family in the summer. She had had symptoms of anxiety as well as depression and found travelling very difficult. She experienced anxiety symptoms sometimes just travelling to town on the bus. With the clinician Lufti worked on understanding her anxiety symptoms and undertook some graded practice. As part of this she relabelled her anxiety symptoms as excitement as well as challenging her anxious thoughts.

Positive self-statements

This is another coping technique designed to shift the young person's focus to positive experiences. It involves building up positive beliefs about self that the young person can agree and using these to build confidence for more challenging difficulties.

> *Louise age 16 believed that she would never find a boyfriend as no one would ever like her. She was able to think about girl friends that she had recently got to know as she had joined the local gym and developed positive self-statements about her ability to meet new people.*

Re-attribution

A common cognitive pattern in depression involves incorrectly assigning the blame or responsibility for adverse events to oneself. Depressed young people are particularly prone to blaming themselves. 'Re-attribution' can be used when a young person unrealistically blames themselves for occurrences.

The clinician and young person review the relevant events and make an appropriate assignment of responsibility. The aim is not to absolve the young person of all responsibility but to look at all the factors contributing to an adverse experience. Thus the way may be opened for applying objective problem-solving techniques and a search for solutions.

> *Dawn, a 14-year-old girl who had developed a depressive illness had been sexually abused by her stepfather. She came to her session saying that she felt that all the family's difficulties were her fault.*
>
> *Dawn:*   *My mum is unhappy, my dad is in prison, all because of what I did.*
> *Therapist:* *What have you done wrong?*
> *Dawn:*   *I told about what my dad did.*
> *Therapist:* *Can you remember that decision?*
> *Dawn:*   *Yes, I was very very scared and unhappy and I couldn't bear it any longer.*
> *Therapist:* *At the time your telling was the only thing you could have done. What has happened since may have happened anyway. I understand how you feel but I'd like us to think about the things that have happened since, separately from your 'decision'.*

When the clinician and young person talked about her feelings and thoughts Dawn was helped by the method of re-attribution that is identifying the cause of the difficulty as residing outside of herself. The clinician and young person went on to talk about the changes that had occurred following disclosure and her stepfather's responsibility. Dawn's cognitions of self-blame may be countered by reviewing the facts of the events that resulted in self-criticism and challenging the belief that the young person is 100% responsible for any negative consequences.

Alternative explanations

Depressed young people may perceive their problems as insoluble. If appropriate, work on social problem-solving can be introduced and the concepts developed to involve other interpretations or solutions to the young person's problems.

The clinician should not be diverted by the young persons' claims that they have 'tried everything'. Although depressed people sincerely believe that they have explored every possible option, it is more likely that they will have automatically rejected several options and stopped the search for others because they have made a prejudgement that the problem is insoluble. Searching for alternative explanations provides another approach to insoluble problems.

> *Tina, age 15 years, was convinced that she was unlikeable and would never have any friends. As evidence she told the clinician about having overheard two classmates talking about her, and saying that she was boring and miserable. The clinician elicited two points. Tina had been depressed at the time this conversation took place, and so it was possible that she was not behaving as normal. Also she did not like these particular classmates, whom she knew to be spiteful, and so their opinion did not really matter. The clinician encouraged Tina to examine her beliefs in the light of these. Following this the clinician and Tina discussed other situations where Tina felt that she had been more socially successful.*

Specific challenging negative thinking techniques include:

- detection of automatic thoughts (continuation of previous work)
- examination and reality testing
- re-attribution techniques
- finding alternative solutions.

Emotional first aid

Talking about negative feelings and thoughts may be distressing. The following distraction techniques can help to reduce depressive thinking and ruminations. These can be used within session if the young person needs to feel more in emotional control. Demonstration and practice within sessions will be needed for the young person to learn the techniques.

Focus on an object: Look at something, anything will do and describe its shape, colour, number of corners and other features to yourself. As a first step describe these aloud to me. Once you have the idea you can say the description to yourself.

Sensory awareness: Concentrate and be aware of what is going on around you. Pay attention to sounds in particular. Try to describe them.

Thought stopping: First identify a positive thought or image, for instance a holiday experience. Note each negative thought or feeling and each time it arises say 'stop' to yourself and switch to the positive thought or image.

These techniques have features in common with mindfulness.

> Emotional first aid aims to help in emotional control. The clinician can teach distraction techniques:
>
> * focus on an object
> * sensory awareness
> * thought stopping.

Mindfulness

Mindfulness is a psychological treatment successfully used with depressed adults. It is based on meditation techniques and involves paying attention in a specific way. The intention is to be focused on the present moment and oneself in relation to it. This can assist in responding to events with full awareness of automatic tendencies and hence allow the individual to exercise a choice to respond differently. This should result in a decreased emotional reactivity and vulnerability. For instance an individual might recognise a negative automatic thought but instead of reacting to the thought recognise it as something that is potentially a problem but not necessarily so. To date, there has been limited application with young people of this promising technique (Thompson and Gauntlett-Gilbert, 2008).

Levels of cognitive intervention

Young people vary in their ability to engage with cognitive techniques. For some the development of awareness of their negative thoughts is helpful but challenging the thoughts is difficult. For this group the focus will need to be on developing positive self-statements that promote effective coping and examining the disadvantages of negative thinking.

Jenny frequently identified the thought 'I am rubbish' but struggled with cognitive restructuring. She learned to notice the thought and the negative feelings that went with it and to substitute several positive thoughts as a distraction.

Some young people will be able to describe more elaborate negative thoughts. For these it is possible to challenge the thoughts by examining the evidence and developing more adaptive and realistic appraisals as described in earlier sections. They may also be able to understand and recognise the irrational thinking processes that lead to the thoughts.

At a further level it may be possible to examine the core beliefs that are driving the thoughts for instance, 'no one will ever love me', and challenge these. Work with all elements of thinking is likely to be helpful and the approach will need to be guided by what the young person is able to achieve using as many examples as is realistic.

Continuing cognitive work

Working on cognitive challenging is likely to continue over several sessions. The sessions generally follow a pattern of the young person bringing in thought records about specific difficult incidents during the week that are then discussed in detail in the session with reference to previous work and handouts. The young person becomes more adept at challenging themselves and may be able to use records that invite them to do this (see Thought Challenging Worksheet). Others will require the clinician's assistance and will bring material describing only events, thoughts and feelings. As the young person's mood improves typically fewer episodes are recorded and the clinician can identify situations that arose which did not lead to negative thinking but would have done so in the past.

As with activity scheduling, the clinician can continue with home practice of thought recording and review while moving on to other areas within sessions.

> Cognitive work takes place over a series of sessions.
>
> It is useful to continue thought recording even when the session content has moved on to other areas.

7

General cognitive behavioural techniques

This chapter will describe some useful cognitive behaviour therapy (CBT) techniques that can be used for problems common among depressed young people including working with communication and interpersonal skills and social problem-solving. Often depressive symptoms will have led to difficulties in social relationships such as break ups with friends. Problem-solving can help in identifying and tackling other issues. Improvements in social skills and social relationships can help mood to be further improved. Development of these techniques will take several sessions.

Enhancing communication and interpersonal skills

It is well established that depressive symptoms in adolescents are strongly associated with impairment of interpersonal relationships with peers, parents and teachers. The goal of social skills training is to improve the social interaction and social competence of young people. Social skills can be addressed at several different levels, from micro-skills such as appropriate eye contact to more complex skills such as being able to join in an activity or seek help from a teacher. Other social difficulties may be cognitive such as misperceiving others' intentions or planning how to deal with a difficult situation. There is an extensive research literature exploring the effectiveness of targeted interventions with children with social skills problems, showing mixed results (Donovan and Spence, 2005). Readers seeking more extensive details of social skills training are referred to the Spence (1995) therapy manual.

Within Lewinsohn's depression model, social skills deficits are seen as a factor in lack of social reinforcement. There have been several studies using social skills training as a therapeutic intervention for depressed adolescents. There is also evidence that poor peer relationships predict poor outcome in adolescent depressive disorders. Clarke and Lewinsohn's group intervention for depression includes social skills and problem-solving components (Clarke *et al.*, 1990).

Many depressed people report an overwhelming number of self-debasing and negative cognitions at times when they are socially and physically inactive. They criticise themselves for avoiding other people. This can cause increasing passivity and social isolation. This may be addressed, in part, by activity scheduling. However, if the young person has more global social difficulties then the activities taken up may have involved restricted social activities or solitary pursuits. This can indicate that social skills training may be required once the young person is feeling less depressed and more confident. Young people often have a treatment goal of improving social relationships for instance making new friends. A social situation checklist can be used to identify specific areas of difficulty (Spence, 1995).

Often the first step of a social skills intervention involves helping the young person to improve basic communication skills. This might include:

- listening to others
- starting a conversation
- continuing a conversation
- introducing themselves.

Once this has been completed or when the clinician is satisfied that the young person is competently using these skills, work on more difficult interpersonal skills can take place. This might include:

- joining in with more than one person
- sharing
- complimenting
- helping others
- asking someone for a date.

Clinicians prompt sheets for these sessions can be found in the Materials and worksheets.

Aims of working on communication and social skills:

- to tackle social withdrawal and social isolation in continuation with work on activity scheduling
- to give the young person the message that the skills can be learnt
- to link improvement in social relationships with improved mood.

Use of role play

Role play is a very useful technique. It is important to practise before trying to use the exercises in sessions, so that they can be informally introduced. The aim is to introduce the role play in the normal flow of conversation. For example 'So, imagine that I'm a friend of yours and I say . . .'

Important practical aspects of role play include:

- keep the role play practice brief and to the point
- make sure that the young person understands the purpose
- make sure that the young person succeeds
- always reflect back on the positives and practise the weaker points again
- use a sense of humour
- demonstrate an accepting and non-judgemental approach.

The clinician can take the lead, use humour and have fun by perhaps demonstrating the 'wrong way' in an extreme fashion and then asking the young person to identify what was wrong. The young person and clinician can then identify better options.

A useful strategy is to let the young person 'relive' a situation that they have identified as difficult. Practice in playing different roles can be useful in thinking about alternative perspectives.

Therapist: Ok, it sounds to me like that was a difficult social situation and you wish you had dealt with it better. Why don't I pretend to be your friend and you can try another approach to see if it would have ended more the way you hoped?

If the young person is not happy with the outcome the clinician can suggest and model other options.

The young person is also given the opportunity to explore more adaptive ways of thinking and relating to others. The clinician can start with a general statement such as 'Young people often have difficulties in getting on with other people and sorting out everyday problems with others. These difficulties have an effect on their mood by making them feel even more sad'.

A handout can be used as a basis for discussion, highlighting the main features of listening and conversation skills (see Box).

Listening skills:

- ***stop*** and look at the person who is talking

- ***pay attention*** to what they are saying

- ***wait*** until it is your turn

- then ***answer***, reflect back what they said and comment from your own experiences.

Conversation skills:

- find someone you want to talk to
- stop and think of something to say
- go over to the person
- say 'hello' and start talking in a friendly way
- take turns talking
- ending the conversation or say 'Goodbye'.

Introducing myself:

- ***think***
- go over
- say your name
- ask their name
- start a conversation.

Interpersonal skills

The clinician can explain that learning to talk and get on better with friends, parents and teachers can be helpful. The young person is asked to offer two recent examples of difficulties with communication for instance, arguments, scared to talk to people, difficulty making new friends. Information in a handout can be used to explore difficulties in each area, using role play.

Joining in:

- think
- go over
- ask to join in.

Sharing:

- ***think*** whether you want to share (advantages/disadvantages)
- ***ask*** if he/she/they want to share
- ***share fairly***.

Giving a compliment:

- think about something nice to say that is truthful
- look at the person
- say something nice.

Receiving a compliment:

- look at the person speaking
- say 'Thank you'
- tell more about it if you want to.

Helping others:

- *think* about whether help is needed
- *ask* if help is needed
- *help* if needed.

Home practice

The home practice task will depend on the work covered in the session and on the young person's individual difficulties. The young person might be asked to initiate one conversation per day over the coming week and record these in their diary. In addition, the clinician might explore the potential for the young person to meet new people, introduce themselves and use other interpersonal skills practised in the session. The young person may be asked to pay attention to arguments over the week with parents, peers, teachers and to record these in the diary. The aim is to encourage the young person to monitor and record difficulties with social relationships. In reviewing home practice it is important to reinforce the positive elements and practise and model areas of difficulty.

Mary's (aged 15) church had a youth club that she attended. She saw this as an opportunity to make friends but she did not feel that she knew how to start a conversation. Mary and the clinician practised this several times and took turns in the roles. Mary started to get ideas about what worked best for her. She decided she would walk up to someone that she thought looked friendly, smile and make eye contact. If they smiled and made eye contact back she felt this would be a good sign. She would then introduce herself and ask what school they went to.

Sarah (aged 13) was looked after by the local authority and lived in a small children's home. She found it particularly difficult to accept praise or compliments. The clinician had observed this in sessions when trying to praise Sarah for her hard work. In the social skills session the clinician raised this. Sarah said that praise made her feel embarrassed. The clinician asked how it felt if someone did not accept her compliment. She had never considered this so the clinician and Sarah role played an example. Sarah played the clinician and the clinician a teenager. Sarah gave the teenager a compliment and the 'teenager' gave a lengthy refusal of the compliment. Out of role the clinician asked Sarah how she felt. She replied that it was annoying, that she would not have given a compliment unless she meant it and it put her off giving any more. The clinician and Sarah repeated the role play and the teenager accepted the compliment a little reluctantly. Sarah decided to practise this at home with her key worker. The following week she had many examples and said it felt nice to be complimented by a teacher and her key worker. The clinician noticed that Sarah started to accept praise and give the clinician positive feedback on the sessions.

Problem-solving

Problem-solving can be used to work on interpersonal skills, helping the young person to find ways of dealing with everyday difficulties in getting on with others.

> Problem-solving involves:
>
> * identifying problems
> * thinking of various solutions (brainstorming)
> * examining the pros and cons of each solution
> * putting the solution into action in role play first.

This work may be used to follow or precede sessions on communication and interpersonal skills. Although the majority of depressed young people are expected to have impaired psycho-social functioning, its causes and characteristics will vary. Some may have effective social skills but show impaired problem-solving. The young person is also likely to benefit from constructive and supportive discussions about addressing problems. Social difficulties will often be related to a degree of low self-esteem, negative thinking and depressed mood. It is therefore important for the clinician to keep working on mood–cognition–behaviour links. This approach can be helpful with young people who have found working cognitively difficult as the more practical nature of the sessions may generate thoughts that were previously inaccessible.

Work is focused on 'here and now' difficult situations. By experiencing success it is hoped that the young person may generalise and create a new pattern in interpersonal relationships. The link between successful completion of social tasks and improved mood can be demonstrated.

Aims of problem-solving.

1   To help the young person clarify specific ways of approaching social and interpersonal problems. It is important to highlight the notion of 'small everyday problems' rather than major crises or life events since these are within the young person's ability to change.
2   To link improvement in social relationships with mood.
3   To combine work on communication and interpersonal skills with inter-personal problem-solving.

Many young people are overwhelmed by the scale of their problems. It is therefore important to choose a problem to work on which is potentially easily solvable, and for which the goal is realistic and specific. This requires judgement from the clinician.

Depressed young people often find it difficult to generate solutions. Suggesting more absurd solutions as well as sensible ones can often help to free up discussion. Young people with low mood are likely to disqualify any of their successes. It is therefore important that the clinician is very positive about any attainment of goals and problem-solving processes. This task may provide a useful context within which to identify and challenge a young person's negative attitudes about both themselves and their ability to sort out problems.

The handouts on problem-solving and accompanying worksheet can be a useful focus for the session (see Materials and worksheets). The clinician can take the young person step by step through the process.

Seven steps to solving problems

1   Define the problem.
      What exactly is the problem? Make it fit into '. . . the problem is how to. . .'
2   Brainstorm to generate possible solutions.
      Think of as many ways you can of solving this problem.
3   Focus energy and attention on the task.
      Be determined to solve this problem – don't let it beat you. Be sure of why it is important to solve the problem.
4   Project the outcome of each of the possible solutions.

> *What would be the advantages and disadvantages of doing each of the things you outlined in Step 2?*
>
> 5   Weigh the consequences and choose a solution.
>
>   *Step 4 can take some time! Weigh up the pros and cons and choose a solution to try for starters.*
>
> 6   Evaluation the outcome of the chosen action.
>
>   *See what happens!*
>
> 7   Give yourself a reward for success or try one of the other possible solutions.
>
>   *If you got it right the first time, well done! Give yourself a treat. If not, don't be too disappointed – work your way through your list and try another solution or go back to the start and re-define the problem.*

Use the previous week's diary to choose a problem situation. The young person is asked to clarify which particular aspect of this situation or inter-action they found most difficult and to brainstorm options. Alternatively the young person can choose a social situation in which they encounter difficulties. The young person and clinician then work through the seven steps, repeating with another problem if necessary. It may be helpful to use more general problems if the young person has difficulty in finding suitable personal examples. This can be particularly useful if there are extensive difficulties that the young person is not able to acknowledge. A list of social problem-solving predicaments is included in the Materials and worksheets.

It is important to take a non-judgemental approach about the various options young people offer and to praise them for coming up with any ideas. This first case example below demonstrates this. It may be the case that the young person comes up with options first that do not work in real life but seem to use them again and again anyway. This experience just reinforces their negative thoughts.

The clinician should encourage the young person to write all of the options down. It is important to be aware that facial expressions or body language may suggest disapproval of some of the options and it is important for the clinician to remain neutral. The more acceptable options may need encouragement for instance apologising or ignoring. The young person needs to take ownership of the options and must not feel that the clinician is nagging, advising, parenting or counselling. None of these will produce the desired outcome. The aim is to increase the young person's insight into the fact there are always options in any given situation. If they take ownership they will be keen to try out new ways as homework.

Therapist: *This session is about social problem-solving. We have noticed that your mood has been affected by falling out with your friends. Let's look in your diary and see if we can identify a problem to work on.*

Emma: *I fell out with my best friend Jenny on Monday. She was talking about me to another girl. We have not spoken since.*

Therapist:	*Let's work through the model with that one then.*
Emma:	*Ok.*
Therapist:	*What is the problem?*
Emma:	*I argued with my best friend.*
Therapist:	*What is the goal here?*
Emma:	*I would like to make up and be friends again.*
Therapist:	*Ok. Let's do a brainstorm of all the ideas we can think of that may be options to reach that goal. Can you think of one?*
Emma:	*I could go get a girl to beat her up.*
Therapist:	*That could be an option. Any others?*
Emma:	*Apologise?*
Therapist:	*That is another one. Any more ideas?*
Emma:	*Get my mum to ring her mum.*
Therapist:	*Good. You are doing well at making this list of options. What else?*
Emma:	*Write a letter?*
Therapist:	*Great. You have four now. Any more?*
Emma:	*(she sits in silence)*
Therapist:	*How about just leaving it? Would that be an option?*
Emma:	*Yes, I could.*
Therapist:	*Ok. We have five options now. That is probably enough so what is the next step?*
Emma:	*(reads from handout): Project the outcomes of each option.*
Therapist:	*Let's pick one.*
Emma:	*Apologise?*
Therapist:	*What would be involved in that?*
Emma:	*I wouldn't do it!*
Therapist:	*Ok. Just say you did, what would be involved?*
Emma:	*I would phone and we would talk and I would apologise.*
Therapist:	*What would be the advantages of that?*
Emma:	*It would solve it.*
Therapist:	*Any other advantages?*
Emma:	*We would be best friends again.*
Therapist:	*Looks good. What are the disadvantages?*
Emma:	*I would have admitted that I was wrong.*
Therapist:	*Are there other disadvantages?*
Emma:	*She will always want me to give in when we have an argument.*
Therapist:	*Would it be very hard to do?*
Emma:	*Very hard.*
Therapist:	*We need to do this for all the options and then you would need to choose one as home practice and try it. If it does not help try another one.*

Martin (age 13) was involved in the drama department at his school and had a crush on a 17-year-old girl who was usually the star of any school play. She was very popular. Martin had written a letter to her to tell her he loved her. Before he sent it he showed it to his clinician and asked if the clinician thought this was a good idea. The clinician suggested that they work through all the options and look at the pros and cons of each.

Martin came up with the options of: write a letter, tell her in person, tell her friend, do nothing and flirt with her and see if she flirts back. Martin worked through the options and wrote down the pros and cons of each. The pro of all of them except 'do nothing' was that she might love him too. The cons seemed to be extensive and included: she will laugh at me, others will laugh at me, she may not love me and I will be publicly humiliated when she turns me down. The worst for Martin was the thought of the letter being passed around school. The clinician then asked what he thought he should do. Martin tore up the letter and said that the risks were too high so he was not going to do anything. Also he reflected that she had an 18-year-old boyfriend and maybe he was too young for her.

John (aged 13) had been referred to the specialist mental health service with depressive symptoms and conduct problems. He was doing well in therapy and actively engaged in sessions. One week he put on the agenda his problem with his English teacher. John was upset that whenever anyone was messing about in class she always jumped to the conclusion that it was him. He admitted that sometimes he was responsible. Regardless of this she would always tell him off. His response was to argue back and leave the classroom. John felt he could not lose face with his mates and let the teacher talk to him like that so he had to leave. He was actually at fault less and less often now and wanted to do better at school. The clinician and John worked through the seven steps of social problem-solving. At the end of this process John chose an option as home practice.

The following week in therapy John was looking very pleased with himself and was eager to put 'feedback on home practice' on the agenda. John said that at the next English lesson another boy had thrown a ball of paper at the teacher's back. She automatically yelled at John. John very politely said 'It was not me Miss!' She looked at him shocked and then replied 'You know John you are right. It cannot always be you and I am sorry that I always accuse you!' John smiled at her and as he did not have to march out of the class to save face he continued with his work. He said that after that his mates still thought he was cool but the cycle had been broken. He was so pleased he rolled up his sleeves and said he had some other problems that he wanted to work on.

Nathan (aged 11) had worked on a problem and was not happy with the outcome of the option that he chose. He had never met his father who had opted out of his life before he was born but his grandparents sent cards, letters and gifts. He had negotiated with his mother that if he received a letter from his paternal grandparents, he, rather than his mother, would open it as it was his letter. Then he would talk to his mum if the letter upset him. A letter came as expected a few weeks later in time for his birthday. The contents of the letter upset Nathan. He went back to his list of options and decided in future his mother would open the letter and share it if appropriate. She would take action with the grandparents if needed. This seemed like a good choice as Nathan planned it with his mother. Situations such as this will often require work with parents, carers or other adults involved in the young person's life.

8

Ending therapy

At the start of therapy a process of assessment and review was negotiated. The approximate number of sessions is usually forecast. Regular use of mood rating scales and questionnaire measures used in the initial assessment will have demonstrated the pattern of progress in addition to reports from the young person and their parents or carers. In an ideal world the end of therapy would always occur when the young person and clinician agree with parents about the successful and sustained achievement of shared goals, following a suitable period of follow-up. There would be supporting evidence from a teacher about improved progress in school. In reality, endings are often more complex.

Planning ahead for ending

It is important to plan ahead for ending, even if all treatment goals are not fully achieved. The final sessions should always be positive. This is helped by discussing and planning the anticipated total number of sessions and by regular review. By being very open and transparent in the contracting of the therapy the young person is always aware that therapy is time limited. The clinician wants to avoid the ending of therapy as being perceived as a loss (of the relationship) or a reflection of having failed. These are common themes in depressive thinking.

Therapy should end gradually, with decreasing frequency of sessions. Doubts and concerns about ending therapy should be discussed and a plan made. Cognitive techniques may be helpful here. Openly asking the young person how many more sessions they think they may need can help to assess their feelings about ending therapy as well as checking if they see themselves as making progress.

Wind down sessions can be planned with increasing emphasis on the young person's actions that have resulted in progress, linking in with original problems, de-emphasising the clinician's role and promoting the young person's competence and control in achieving positive changes. The clinician's activity in suggesting home practice tasks can be reduced over time, with the young person increasingly taking responsibility for generating their own.

It is important to discuss likely threats to relapse (for instance stressors such as school examinations) and that the new skills learned will deal effectively with any re-emergence of symptoms. This involves relapse prevention planning.

Final session

As part of ending the clinician encourages the young person to reflect on the different stages of treatment and see that change does not occur all at once. Often the young person will have forgotten how things were at the outset so looking back over diaries and worksheets may help with this. It may be necessary to acknowledge any problems not yet solved but which may improve with time.

If unresolved difficulties are still of high concern and there are no signs of improvement (for instance school-related problems), the clinician may need to identify alternative sources of support. This will usually involve convening a planning meeting including the young person, their parents or carers and any other professionals involved.

It is useful to go through the session content in some detail using the following format.

Review of CBT

- General review of current situation.
- Discussion of initial objectives.
- Outstanding problems.
- Review of strategies used, what helped:
  - recognition of emotion
  - links between events feelings thoughts
  - self-rewards
  - problem-solving
  - detecting automatic thoughts
  - examining and challenging behaviours.
- Review of meetings:
  - individual sessions
  - family meetings
  - school liaison

> ○   other treatments.
> ● Re-rate goals.
> ● Establish young person's view of ways forward.

Most young people will identify some therapeutic topics as having been more useful than others. The clinician attempts to enable the young person to focus as specifically as possible on the process of improvement and to reinforce their sense of self-control. At the same time, the clinician repeats the message that if problems arise in the future the young person can start to use some of these techniques again.

The clinician should use closing sessions to write jointly with the young person a summary of the sessions and what has been helpful. Putting these ideas in a therapeutic letter or 'blueprint' can be helpful for the young person. This should include an outline of how and when to get in contact again if there are future problems, shared as appropriate with parents and carers. A standard format and clinician prompt sheet is included in the Materials and worksheets.

Towards the conclusion of therapy, it is not unusual for young people to re-visit the causes or triggers for their difficulties. Reviewing the formulation and considering past influences and events are likely to be an important aspect of ending therapy. Relapse prevention work can be reassuring.

> **Relapse prevention**
> ● Discuss cognitive formulation.
> ● Triggers of depressive episode.
> ● Strategies that have helped in recovery.
> ● Early warning signs, what were the first signs of difficulties?
> ● Crisis plan – how to get help, what to do, who to involve.

Sometimes young people drop out and stop attending once they start to feel better. This can often involve a succession of cancelled appointments. It may be useful to write to the young person, offer to meet to review and provide contact details for the future.

Booster sessions

Booster sessions can be used at longer intervals to assist in wind down with young people who have been identified as vulnerable to relapse. This will be likely to lead to repetition in session content, particularly in the clinician encouraging the young person to evaluate appropriately their ability to deal with problems as they arise. Cognitive techniques can be used to challenge negative thoughts about relapse.

> Booster sessions can be scheduled at monthly intervals to allow monitoring of problems and further revision of effective strategies.

Darryl's (age 13) depressive symptoms improved substantially after 12 sessions. He gave himself a mood score of 9/10 (with 1 the score at the time of referral). The environmental stressor (his father's chronic physical illness) was still present and acting as a maintaining factor. When Darryl was asked about the components of CBT that had helped, he could not identify any particular factors. He was enjoying being 'treated by his mother'. He had not been very compliant with the practice and had not been using the diary for most of the sessions. These related to his difficulties with reading. He seemed to use the principles from the sessions. The clinician attributed his improvement mainly to making links between his mood and thoughts with his father's illness, which occurred early in therapy. This was written into a therapy blueprint. Monthly follow-up appointments were arranged. The clinician also made some joint plans with his social worker to support the family, to encourage Darryl to develop peer relationships and participate in constructive activities which might act as protective factors in a future family crisis.

Gaynor's (age 13) anxiety and depressive symptoms were subjectively much improved by the end of treatment. Her mother, who was still moderately depressed, still encouraged Gaynor to come into the parental bedroom at night, and felt that Gaynor was little better. The clinician emphasised to the mother the gains that Gaynor had made and reassured her that contact would be maintained and further CBT offered if Gaynor felt worse. It seemed that some of Gaynor's difficulties in separating from her mother were encouraged by mother, whose relationship with her father had become progressively worse. Work on the marital relationship had been resisted by Gaynor's parents.

Gaynor had always worked very hard during the treatment sessions, and had kept her diary very carefully. She was encouraged to continue with her diary and to monitor her thoughts. She was advised to use 'what's the evidence' whenever she became anxious in social situations. At follow-up, three months later she remained well and was discharged from the clinic.

The clinician defines and repeats the main themes of the treatment to the young person and links them to the formulation. A therapy 'blueprint' may be used to describe what has been discussed.

9

Working with the wider system

Working with parents

Working with the young person within their life context is widely recognised as good practice from assessment through to intervention. Parents are frequently the help-seeking agents on behalf of their children and will be involved from the outset. However, parental behaviour or difficulties may be seen as instrumental in the development or maintenance of their children's depression.

> **Key issues**
>
> - Psycho-education: sharing diagnosis and formulation.
> - Family element in formulation.
> - Differing goals.
> - Confidentiality.
> - Parental role in therapy.
> - Evaluation of progress.
> - Parents with affective disorders.
> - One clinician or two?
> - Parental mental health issues.
> - Relapse prevention.

Wolpert *et al.* (2005) identify three clinical challenges in using individual cognitive behaviour therapy (CBT) with children and adolescents. These are balancing viewpoints, where there may be differences within the family about treatment goals; addressing family issues where underlying family problems may need addressing; and promoting genuine collaboration with both the young person and with parents such that the role that parents can play in the intervention is acknowledged.

Wolpert also described a range of possible configurations of parental involvement. The parent can be seen as a facilitator (child offered individual CBT with the parent not present or infrequently seen). This is most suited where there is an older adolescent who is motivated and where the family is supportive and where there are no major family issues. This is very similar to models of working with adults. Where parents are more actively involved in supporting therapy some authors have considered them to be co-clinicians (Stallard, 2002). Alternatively parents may be targeted in their own right, most commonly in parent training programmes or similar interventions for conduct disorder and behaviour problems. This may also be considered where there are complex family factors in the presenting problems.

Working with parents to support individual CBT

Parents need to understand:

- the nature of the young person's problems as assessed by the clinician
- the aims and methods of CBT in relation to young person and family problems
- how they may assist with specific goals for instance, providing permission and support for particular activities.

Parents will need to be involved in goals that aim to influence their relationship with the young person. For instance, it may be desirable to increase the time that the family spends together in positive activities in order to reduce the young person's social isolation. Parents also can provide some external corroboration of the young person's progress although the young person's view will be most important.

It is important to remember that working to shared goals with the young person does not automatically involve working to shared goals with family members. It is important that goals are agreed with the young person that are not reliant on the compliance of others. Care is likely to be needed in including parents where, for instance, their major concern is the young person's behaviour at home or antisocial activities when these are not the major focus of CBT. Parents may struggle to be supportive when they do not share the clinician's formulation of the young person's difficulties.

Clare's parents were very concerned about her angry outbursts and her lack of contact with the family. They found her very difficult and all attempts to speak to her seemed to result in rows. They wanted her back to her old sociable self and thought that she was choosing to be awkward and difficult as a result of contact with antisocial friends. They did not recognise that she was depressed and refused to acknowledge her mood swings and irritability. Individual work with Clare commenced despite the parents' views. They were clear that she needed individual help to change. However, their attitudes and negative cognitions became increasingly problematic and the clinician chose to involve another worker to work with them on the basis of Clare's difficulties.

Everyone involved also needs to be clear about boundaries of confidentiality (see also p. 29). The clinician should always consider including the young person in any discussion with parents. Such discussions provide opportunities for checking out a young person's understanding, negotiating pitfalls and establishing clearly what parents hear about the content of sessions. The main danger is of parents being undermining of the young person's progress, but at least this is clearly brought to the clinician's awareness. Parents who feel guilty about their child's difficulties can be helped to feel part of the solution by focusing on the here and now and considering ways forward rather than how the young person's depressed situation came about. Some parents may need clear rules about how they contact the clinician outside sessions and the consequences.

Parents' role in formulation

Beck's formulation of depressive schemata as developing from early experience implies a role for parents. Thus clinicians working with young people are faced with working with parents possibly both as part of the problem and part of the solution. Difficult experiences for parents early in a child's life may have compromised the development of a secure attachment. The parents may themselves have experienced losses at crucial stages of the child's development making them less emotionally available. Child mental health practitioners are experienced in applying attachment theory to the understanding of parents' relationships with children. They can appraise relationships within an attachment framework, consider the developmental course of symptoms within the family and potentially intervene on this basis (Crittenden, 2005).

There have been many research studies demonstrating inter-generational links between depressed parents, most commonly mothers, and the increased risk of depression in their children (Radke-Yarrow, 1998). Mediating and moderating variables are unclear and there are likely to be many contributory factors. A recent study (Simmons *et al.*, 2006) compared schema of depressed young women (age 13–17 years) with their mothers and showed a relationship between depressed mothers and daughters in mood and negative schema that was not present for a control group of young people not accessing specialist mental health services and their mothers. This raises the possibility that depressed mood and associated cognitions in mothers may have an influence on development of depression in their daughters. However, no conclusions can be drawn about the direction of causality nor if a third factor influences both.

In order to clarify the direction of causality, a study compared mother–

child interaction in families with a young person who was either currently depressed, at high risk of developing depression or in a healthy control group (Dietz *et al.*, 2008). Performance in a standardised problem-solving interaction showed that mothers of depressed young people showed less control and were more disengaged from their child. The high-risk group showed similar scores on these variables, significantly different from those of the control group. Scores on both measures were higher if the mothers had histories of depression themselves. High rates of negativity and low rates of positive behaviour were demonstrated from depressed young people, unlike the high-risk and healthy groups. The authors concluded that the bi-directional effects of maternal disengagement and low levels of positive behaviour from the young person are likely to precede the development of depression and serve as risk factors for recurrent depressive episodes. These studies make a strong case for interventions that promote positive affective exchanges between parents and young people and increased parental involvement in parallel with individual work with the young person.

In clinical practice it is often the case that the clinician is dealing with a depressed young person and a depressed parent therapeutically, regardless of causality. It is important that this is not viewed by parents as blaming. Parents feel responsible for their children's difficulties and developing formulations that are blaming is unhelpful. Parents rarely have direct control over life events and relationship difficulties that may directly or indirectly have an impact on the mental health of all family members. Prompt treatment of concurrent parental depression may increase a parent's positive involvement with their child and allow them to be more active participants in their child's treatment.

Treating a parent for depression

It is important to consider that it is likely that one or both parents may have previous or current experience of depression. They may not recognise the similar symptoms in their child or they may over-identify and make erroneous assumptions about the young person's experience. They may have very particular views from their own experience about the approach to be taken. Sometimes parents may learn helpful information as a result of the contact from their child's treatment and apply the work to their own difficulties. It may be useful to recommend self-help materials for adults (there are a wide range of books and guides for adults using CBT in addition to interactive computerised programmes such as Beating the Blues available in many primary health care settings) or prompt referral to adult mental health services. The parent should not be treated by the same clinician as their child.

The clinician may need to support parents who experience guilt, have awareness of their own over-involvement, or projection of their own symptoms, in finding alternative ways of coping that support positive change for their child. Conversely the young person's understanding of the formulation may be assisted by discussing family life experiences for instance bereavement or separation together with a parent.

Max's mother had died when he was aged 7. His father had experienced depressive episodes for the 3 following years and received counselling that had been helpful. At age 15 Max became depressed after his older brother left home for university. His father had a new partner. Max's father sought individual therapy for Max, as he had found this helpful himself. Max made good progress with CBT but this was accelerated when it was possible to include his father actively in sessions that recalled the circumstances of his mother's loss and his father's depression. Max was able to make a more meaningful formulation about the impact of the family bereavement and his felt need to stand on his own feet in the face of difficulty.

A recent development in CBT practice with children and families involves conjoint sessions in development of a systemic CBT formulation (Dummett, 2006). This involves development of a visual template including the most clinically significant processes in development and maintenance of problems taking into account differing family members' perspectives.

> Parents can help in formulation as therapy progresses.
>
> Issues may arise for parents themselves.
>
> The clinician often needs to help to reduce guilt and sense of blame.

Individual and family sessions

The following provide examples where family work is needed to supplement individual work. In the first case there is a need for parental support to negotiate independence and autonomy following successful treatment for depression.

Sarah, age 15, presented with a 2-year history of depression. She was the younger of two daughters; her mother worked part time as an occupational therapist and her father as a builder. Her older sister Clare had left school recently aged 18, started work and was in a steady relationship with her boyfriend of the past 3 years. Sarah engaged well with CBT and soon was showing no symptoms of depression. She had gained in confidence and regularly resumed going out with a group of friends. She truanted from school on a couple of occasions, having previously attended well and worked hard. At home rows with her parents increased over her staying out late, drinking with friends and within her group, mixing with young men who were several years older. A crisis ensued when in an argument Sarah stormed out and refused to return home, staying with her aunt and cousins for a few days. It was of note that her sister Clare had never presented any similar challenges to her parents, having been less socially active before meeting a boyfriend whom her parents liked. It was necessary to move from individual work with Sarah to joint work with her parents and into a model of working that shifted the focus from Sarah's individual symptoms to relationship problems within the family. This involved her parents thinking about Sarah's increasing autonomy and their own strategies for handling conflict. Sarah did not become depressed again. After two sessions with her parents she refused to attend and further sessions took place with her parents without her. Work involved considering the parents' own experiences of adolescence, realistic boundary setting for teenagers and their expectations of Clare and Sarah.

With some young people it may be important to move from individual to family work and back as a result of issues which emerge, in Uzma's case, dealing with a sense of isolation within the family.

Uzma age 14 was the middle of three children of parents of Pakistani origin. Her father was from the second generation of his family born in the UK. His wife had come from Pakistan to marry him 20 years earlier. Uzma was referred by her school nurse as her teachers and parents were concerned about her poor attendance (lateness), 'attitude problems' with authority figures and falling school performance. On assessment she presented with sleep and appetite disturbance in addition to low mood, social withdrawal and concerns about her appearance. She engaged successfully with CBT. As a result of activity scheduling her isolation within the family became clear. She avoided family meals, slept when she came in from school and sat playing on the computer late into the night. She talked of feeling that her mother did not want her and had a better relationship with her younger sister. There was escalating conflict within the family as her parents tried more actively to get her into school on time. The therapeutic sessions shifted to working on Uzma's relationship with her mother, building shared activities and discussion and to addressing parental disagreement about how to handle Uzma's difficulties such that her father was not always seen as 'soft' and mother as rigid and strict. As Uzma became more integrated into the family it was possible to resume individual sessions.

Although in some situations family therapy may be required, in general more problematic family situations can be assisted by encouraging externalising and reducing personalisation of the problem to the child. Parental beliefs and attributions about problems can be explored using cognitive techniques. Strategies that build up secure and positive parent–child relationships, and develop family communication skills and effective problem-solving will assist positive change.

In some situations joint sessions may be important in challenging core beliefs for the young person, who may discover that a parent's view of their efforts or achievements is more positive than they had imagined.

Family therapy and CBT

Problems may arise from parents being under-involved, overprotective, where there are high levels of family discord or chronic parent–child relationship problems. Where family problems are complex, family therapy may be considered. Another clinician will generally need to be involved although it may be helpful for the CBT clinician to have a role in supporting the young person's perspective in family therapy. Most models of family therapy allow for the possibility of a family member receiving individual work in parallel. It is not possible for the individual clinician to conduct other interventions requiring them to have a different perspective from that of the young person, although in other situations or cases they may well be experienced in family work.

> **Good practice**
>
> The clinician needs to be clear about the balance of individual therapy with the young person and joint work with parents, maintaining the young person's interests as paramount. Parents need a clear formulation, regular up-dating and opportunities to discuss progress without breaching the 'private nature of sessions' and a role promoted as parent and not co-clinician.

Working with alternative care settings

CBT is a problem-focused, here and now approach that involves working to a shared agenda with a young person. It is therefore compatible with other approaches that share these characteristics and where workers are trying to support young people who are experiencing difficulties, for example, supportive work within a school or residential care setting.

Young people who are within the public care system often have complex and troubled backgrounds but can still benefit from CBT. Many of the considerations that arise in working with parents may have a bearing with foster or residential carers but equally the professional nature of the relationship can facilitate effective joint working when emotional and family ties can cause difficulties.

Subject to negotiation with the young person, key workers or foster carers may be involved in supporting home-based practice, having discussions between sessions which support understanding or working on specific tasks with the young person.

John lived in a small residential unit. One symptom of his depression was considerable difficulty in settling to sleep at night. He was frequently in trouble when he got up late at night and woke other residents. Together with his key worker the clinician worked on establishing good sleep routines, including permission to listen to the radio, and keeping a chart of time asleep. A system for staying in his room rather than waking others was the basis for a reward system of extra time out of the unit with his key worker and purchasing drawing materials to support a new interest.

Working with schools

Most depressed young people will have difficulties that have generalised to school or college. This may include impaired concentration leading to lack of completion of homework or a fall off in attainment, behaviour problems and non-attendance. Teachers and other school-based staff such as learning mentors can often provide reliable information on peer group networks and social behaviour. They may also provide experience of trusted adults outside the family. Recruiting an interested teacher may be invaluable in promoting generalisation and supporting the aims of therapy. This will require a face to face meeting that may usefully involve the young person. It is important that school staff understand the impact of the depression and how the symptoms will affect the young person academically and socially. They will also need to understand how treatment focuses on the young person's goals that may not immediately reflect the school's or parents' goals.

Clinicians should avoid setting tasks involving school staff without informing them of the basis of the intervention. Supportive teachers often have the resources for clearly defined, structured interventions particularly if they are designed to be scheduled to a specific time.

Clinicians could also consider school support services such as school nurses and school attendance officers who have regular and frequent input into schools. They, like teachers, may be unwittingly undermining if not actively recruited.

As for other key workers, it is important for the clinician to be clear about goals and the focus of work, promote positive behaviours and explain the CBT model. A teacher may have a key task that can be evaluated and reviewed together with the young person.

Peers

It can be very difficult to promote positive peer group interactions for young people with problems in this area. Group CBT may be considered if resources are available (Clarke *et al.*, 2002). If essential, the clinician needs to consider what groups may be available. Adult-supervised activities are easiest to control but are likely to require involvement on the young person's behalf. It is also important to consider wider systemic issues in bullying and victimisation and the consequences of recruitment of adult support into peer group activities.

Good practice

- Involve all significant adults in supporting goals of CBT. This will involve the usual clinical skills.
- Make clear what supporters can contribute.
- Keep informed of progress and listen to their perspective on the young person's progress.

10

Special issues: bullying, bereavement, trauma and suicidality

Young people with depression commonly have complex difficulties. This chapter addresses areas that may be of particular relevance in the aetiology and presentation of depressive disorders and in the formulation of individualised CBT programmes. Co-morbidity is discussed in detail in Chapter 1.

Bullying

It is a common impression among practitioners that young people present in increasing numbers with incidents of bullying within the peer group being seen as a major precipitating factor in the development of mood disorders. Bullying includes physical aggression or threats. It may involve social exclusion, name calling, telling lies or gossip about the young person or teasing, humiliation and scapegoating. Definitions of bullying within the research literature vary but in general the key factors are considered to include persistence over time and intended victimisation of specific individuals.

There is evidence that bullying is common and more prevalent in primary schools than secondary schools. Whitney and Smith (1993) looked at 6,700 children across primary and secondary schools and found 27% in primary and 10% in secondary schools reported they had been bullied. This reduced to 10% and 4% when asked if the bullying was once a week or more frequent. O'Moore, Kirkham and Smith (1997) report similar findings in Ireland where 31% in primary school and 15% in secondary had been bullied in the previous term.

Assessment

Bullying can make a young person's life miserable. Their self-esteem and concentration may be greatly affected, their academic progress reduced and they may be excluded from their peer group. In young people who develop symptoms of depression as a result of bullying, it would not be unusual to see low mood, sleeping difficulties and suicidal thinking. Somatisation is not uncommon for instance, headaches and stomach aches. Anxiety symptoms may be present including unwillingness to attend school.

It is important to be alert for signs of bullying in a depressed young person. Fear of making the situation worse can often lead young people to suffer in silence and not disclose that they are being bullied. Clinicians need to ask direct questions in assessment. Are there bruises without reasonable explanations? Are their belongings or money missing or damaged? Why would a young person who previously liked school now try to avoid attending? Why are they not progressing at the same rate as before? Why do they seem nervous and frightened now? Are there changes in friendships?

Warning signs of bullying

- School avoidance.
- Change in emotional presentation.
- Evidence of injuries.
- Loss of possessions.
- Change in functioning.
- Social avoidance.
- Symptoms of depression.

The clinician might encourage the parents to be inquisitive. These conversations are best started in a general way for instance raising questions about the young person's views on bullying and how their teachers and school deal with it when it occurs, what policies and strategies are used. Stories or books can be a helpful medium for tackling these issues.

Bullying may be part of the problem in depression and not be identified.

Clinicians should be curious and ask directly about all aspects of peer relationships.

Formulation

When bullying has been an element in the young person's presentation it may be included within formulation in a number of different ways. The impact of the experience will differ in different situations. For instance some young people will have existing vulnerabilities as a result of earlier experiences and for others there may be a more acute traumatic response with a background of previously good adjustment. In this situation a depressive response often results from a number of events at the same time.

> *Joe (age 12) had emotional difficulties from age 8, the time that his parents separated. He had learning difficulties identified at primary school and received additional support. He liked school and had several close friends at primary school. He transferred to secondary school and from the outset was victimised by a group of older boys. This came to light after he came home from school bruised and with torn clothes. He became reluctant to go out at all, complained of headaches and stomach pains and had lost his appetite. Later in individual therapy he was able to talk about how he felt that the negative statements the bullies said to him were all true.*

> *Asha's family moved to a new town following her father's promotion in a large computer company. She had always achieved well at school and was due to take public examinations in a year's time. The family as a whole had difficulty with the change. Finding a new house was a problem with a sale falling through. Her father's new job involved longer working hours. Asha had lost a close network of friends. At her new school she experienced racist abuse soon after she started that was at first successfully addressed by school staff. Asha found a best friend and started enjoying school but as the level of work increased became increasingly tearful and low. She showed sleep problems and her mother noticed that she seemed to have lost weight.*

Focusing on bullying in treatment

Working individually with young people

The clinician must ensure that the bullying has been dealt with effectively and has stopped. Collaboratively the young person and clinician can begin to deal with the symptoms that have developed. Once more general depressive symptoms have been addressed it can be helpful to consider how the bullying occurred in detail. Information gathered in assessment will be useful in developing appropriate strategies and interventions.

Problem-solving (see Chapter 7) can be a useful intervention. Smith *et al.* (1994) suggest that assertiveness training can be used to learn how to deal better with bullying situations and improve self-esteem.

Work with victims of bullying may include:

- challenging NATs specific to experiences
- social problem-solving
- communication and interpersonal skills work with an emphasis on assertiveness.

Working with families

When dealing with situations where bullying has occurred it is important to consider parental concerns about protecting their child, particularly if there has been a lack of communication about what has occurred. They are likely to need support and advice in helping their child to move on positively from these experiences.

Working with schools

It is recognised good practice for schools to operate a whole school approach to bullying. This may include anti-bullying campaigns and procedures. There may be sessions on bullying to raise awareness and provide information on what and who is available in school, including activities that target those involved in bullying which may be organised by the school or brought in from education services such as educational psychologist or behaviour support teams.

School strategies to address bullying

- Assertiveness training.
- Peer mediation.
- Adult mediation.
- Conflict resolution skills.
- Group work.
- Circle time.
- Befriending schemes.
- School watch.
- Support groups.

Bereavement

Many young people will have the experience of losing someone in their family or a close acquaintance. Bereavement is a normal response to loss but increases vulnerability to depression.

Not all children react to a bereavement in the same way. Some show little distress initially or later and this is not necessarily dysfunctional. Some will be very distressed for only a short period and others may have lengthy bereavement processes (Carr, 2002a). There is no ordered process of grief but commonly individuals go through stages of shock, denial, yearning, sadness, anger, anxiety, guilt and acceptance. When in shock the bereaved young person may be stunned by the loss and have poor concentration and their school work may suffer. Denial involves refusal to accept that the death has happened. If they are yearning they may search for the lost person and run away or wander off. Sad children and adolescents present as tearful, have poor concentration, sleep and appetite disturbance and are irritable and socially withdrawn. The anger associated with loss may present as sensitivity to conflict, aggressiveness and temper outbursts with those around them including parents, teachers and friends. Anxiety may involve worries that they or others may die and lead to school refusal with physical symptoms such as headaches or stomach aches. Guilt may occur in that they feel it is their responsibility this person died and self-harm may present. Acceptance is the stage defined as a return to normal functioning.

A young person will be more affected by a death of someone close and who was involved in their daily life. A young person is likely to be more distressed by the loss of a grandmother they saw on most days rather than a grandmother they saw once or twice a year. The impact will also be greater where their daily routine is disturbed by the lack of this person or by the fact the other adults around are distressed such that they struggle to care for the young person and maintain routines. A death that is sudden and/or traumatic will affect everyone including the young person.

In the early stages it is important to tell the young person as soon as possible about the death, answer their questions and reassure them. They may worry about being abandoned or blamed. It may help them to be involved in the cultural and religious preparations. Attending a funeral if they wish to attend, and are prepared for it, may help them accept the death. They may need another way to say good-bye such as visiting a grave, lighting candles or saying prayers. Open communication is best. Adults often try to protect children and adolescents by withholding information. In the longer term continued support and talking will help. There may be periods of anger, sadness or anxiety and the young person will need care.

From about age 12, adolescents grieve similarly to adults, in understanding causality and permanence. Their thinking becomes more flexible and may have their own theories or beliefs about death such as the meaning of life or if there is life after death. Some may have difficulties separating from parents and being independent.

All children who suffer grief may show effects on their feelings, thoughts, behaviour and physical well-being. Such effects are normal and depending on duration and severity are not a sign of a disordered reaction. Silverman and Worden (1993) found that a year after a parental death that 19% of children still showed clinically significant problems with adjustment.

Common thoughts that are usual in the early stages of grieving and disappear after a short time are:

- disbelief, for instance: 'This is a bad dream, mum cannot be dead'
- confusion
- preoccupation with thoughts of the dead person
- sense of presence: 'I can feel they are in my room'
- hallucinations, visual and auditory linked to feeling a sense of presence.

Physical symptoms are common such as head- and stomachaches, reduced energy levels, muscular aches and pains and hyper-sensitivity to bodily sensations.

Behaviours that may be seen include angry outbursts, school refusal, bed wetting, loss of interest in previous activities and people, clinginess and loss of independence.

Risk

The loss of a parent is a significant risk factor for an episode of depression in adolescence or later life. Losing a parent of the same gender particularly for boys, appears to be a particularly significant risk factor. The following are also risk factors for poor adjustment (Herbert, 1996).

- Mental illness in surviving parent.
- Financial difficulties.
- Stability of the home environment before and after the death.
- The coping capacity of the surviving parent.
- The quality of the support system of the family after the death; the absence of a close confiding relationship is significant.
- Circumstances of the death for instance, suicide.
- Relationship problems prior to the death.

Bereavement reactions

- Stages of shock, denial, yearning, sadness, anger and anxiety, guilt and acceptance.
- Similar for adolescents as for adults.
- Loss may be complicated by trauma.
- Vulnerability factors include previous relationship quality and relationships with surviving family.
- Risk of depression later in life.

Bereavement issues in CBT

Assessment

Factors that need to be considered in assessment include the developmental context in order to make sense of the young person's questions and fears. Secondly, children's understanding of death and dying varies depending on cultural and religious beliefs. The assessment will need to consider previous experiences and possibly include knowledge based on real events or on books, films or other experiences.

There will be a major impact of death and loss on the family system. The parents, siblings and extended family may be affected emotionally, physically and behaviourally. Relationships may be strained. Daily routine and care for children may have suffered. The role of the deceased within the family needs to be considered. The family beliefs and communication patterns will have effects, for instance, how a young person is allowed to express distress and if others can hear and respond to it. Sadness may be taboo or represent madness. There may be other social and cultural factors that impact.

Formulation

If an assessment indicates that the young person is depressed following a bereavement then cognitive therapy may be a helpful intervention. Depression is characteristically associated with loss. An early loss may have effects many years later. The formulation should identify any vulnerability factors and what the loss means to the young person. Maintenance factors need to be identified so that coping strategies can be developed. Likely goals of therapy may be to come to terms with their loss and to move on with their life.

Considerations during therapy

Individual work

Depressive ruminations may be a maintaining factor in low mood. In adults there are several cognitive models of grief reactions. Raphael *et al.* (1993) found that stimuli that provoked painful feelings would be avoided and therefore individuals avoided processing the loss. Desensitisation to memories and other stimuli that provoke the distress could help.

Adolescents who are old enough to be aware of the death but not old enough to have developed adult coping strategies will be more vulnerable than adults. This is especially true where there has not been open communication and support, not unusual in cases of suicide for instance. This will be magnified where the relationship with the dead adult was ambivalent or difficult. In individual work negative schemas based on loss issues may be apparent, particularly where there have been several losses; 'everyone I love leaves me' may be a core belief.

Family work

Working with the remaining family may help the young person and the family. Improving communication and creating a new view of the world will be important. Family work may include personal and religious rituals and dealing with ambivalent feelings and educating adults about the young person's experience. Adult family members may require treatment in their own right.

> *Joe's paternal grandmother had died suddenly in a road traffic accident a year before referral. She had played a large part in Joe's life following the separation of his parents 9 years earlier when he was age 4. Joe's behaviour was seen as very difficult ever since she died. He was still very low in mood when he was seen in the clinic. The family's view was that he needed bereavement counselling. However, it became clear that problems were more complex and that the loss was exacerbated by the chronically poor and negative relationship between mother and son that had been mitigated by his grandmother. Joe worked well with individual sessions of CBT. Parallel work took place with his mother to work on parenting skills and relationship building with her son.*

> CBT may be helpful following bereavement.
>
> A careful assessment will be needed to identify wider family issues in the loss.

Responses to trauma

Experience of trauma is sometimes identified in young people presenting with depression. This may be associated with bereavement for instance sudden death of a relative or with the young person's direct or indirect experience for instance being assaulted or witnessing violence to a friend. For some experiences over a period of time may be involved for instance in survivors of intra-familial sexual abuse.

A high degree of co-morbidity between post traumatic stress disorder (PTSD) and depression has been reported both in adults and children (Bolton *et al.*, 2000; Thabet *et al.*, 2004). Mechanisms for the relationship are unclear and may vary between cases. There are likely to be complex processes involving interaction between the effects of direct exposure to trauma, child-related factors such as age and previous emotional problems and environmental factors such as loss of a family member in the same traumatic incident. Research studies have not clearly identified the nature of co-morbidity between disorders. The presence of both disorders may result from overlapping symptoms, or from the development of distinct conditions in response to the same event or one disorder precipitating the other through the effect of mediating variables. For instance the persistence of PTSD symptoms coupled with an accumulation of adversities resulting from the trauma could lead to development of depression. The experience of displacement and the additional stressors of immigration have been found to have an independent impact on child psychopathopology in refugee children (Tousignant *et al.*, 1999).

There is evidence that significant numbers of children will develop PTSD following traumatic events. This is well-established for children surviving natural disasters such as earthquakes, transportation disasters or war (Perrin *et al.*, 2000). Stallard *et al.* (1998) reported that one in three children involved in everyday road traffic accidents was found to suffer from symptoms sufficient to warrant a diagnosis of PTSD. Diagnostic criteria require symptoms indicating the persistent re-experiencing of the trauma, the avoidance of stimuli associated with the trauma and increased arousal following a traumatic event that is outside normal experience. Symptoms may include flashbacks, nightmares, sleep disturbance, poor concentration, hyper-vigilance to threat, avoidance and distress. These may be associated with separation anxiety, psychosomatic complaints such as stomachaches and headaches and with reckless behaviour and accidents.

As for adults, the risk of PTSD in children increases with physical proximity to the trauma, previous trauma exposure and may be greater for girls than boys (Pfefferbaum, 1997). Additionally trauma-related distress in parents increases the risk of children developing PTSD (Smith *et al.*, 2001).

Symptoms if untreated may persist for many years (Yule *et al.*, 2000). When symptoms are not sufficiently extensive to warrant a diagnosis of PTSD the impact of the trauma may still warrant direct intervention with symptoms (Kaminer *et al.*, 2005).

PTSD symptoms involve:

- the persistent re-experiencing of the trauma
- the avoidance of stimuli associated with the trauma and
- increased arousal
- onset following a traumatic event that is outside normal experience.

  These may include flashbacks, nightmares, sleep disturbance, poor concentration, hyper-vigilance to threat and distress.

Cognitive behavioural models have been applied to understand the development and persistence of PTSD. These have been discussed in detail by Meiser-Stedman (2002). There are a small number of outcome studies for treatment of PTSD in children including group and individual CBT interventions (March *et al.*, 1998). In the UK, the National Institute for Health and Clinical Excellence recommended trauma-focused CBT as the treatment of choice (NICE, 2005b). Programmes involve anxiety management, coping with anger, cognitive restructuring, exposure and response prevention (March *et al.*, 1998).

Assessment

When young people present with depressive symptoms the impact of past trauma may not be immediately apparent. Routine interviews should ask for information about difficult events in the young person's life including any experienced by other family members. The possibility of the young person having witnessed domestic violence or violence within the community should be considered.

Enquiry about sleep disturbance should include questions about the content of nightmares and any daytime experiences such as flashbacks or disturbing visual images. Particularly if trauma occurred many years earlier it is not unusual for the young person or parent to assert that the consequences have been overcome.

The influence of trauma on the presentation of depression can include:

- experience of PTSD symptoms
- low self-esteem and sequelae as a result of the traumatic episode, particularly if sexual assault is involved
- avoidance behaviour contributing to social withdrawal
- anger
- impulsive behaviour and risk-taking

In the absence of symptoms involving re-experiencing the trauma the young person may still have cognitions that are directly related. These may include anxiety-related cognitions that lead to avoidance, cognitions about blame or about themselves in relation to the experience ('it happened to me because I deserved it'). Survivor guilt can contribute to reckless behaviour.

For some young people treatment of post traumatic symptoms such as cognitions of self-blame that emerge during treatment may be included within the framework of cognitive restructuring. Sometimes the young person will avoid discussion of traumatic events that can be an indicator of residual difficulties. The therapist will need to use judgement in deciding whether or not to pursue this.

Presence of PTSD symptoms should be considered in the assessment of depression. These can be treated within a CBT framework.

Maria age 14 had on two separate occasions experienced sexual assaults. At age 7 she had been the victim of inappropriate touching by a teenage boy on several occasions over a period of weeks. A year prior to her current presentation with depression she and a friend had been sexually assaulted by two boys with whom they were acquainted. Maria had symptoms of major depressive disorder which improved with CBT such that she was symptom free after 10 sessions. She had previously been referred for counselling in relation to the sexual assaults but had refused to engage after one session because she did not wish to go over past events. She expressed the view to the clinician that she wished to look to the future and that past events were not a problem for her. However, once Maria's depression had improved it seemed to the clinician that she had residual symptoms likely to relate to the sexual assaults. These included a sense of being different from her peers. She was also continuing to experience adverse comments from other young people in the neighbourhood. The clinician decided in the face of her continued refusal to describe what she recalled to work on her confidence in protecting herself in the future. This involved using problem-solving. During the course of this work Maria described cognitions relating to low self-worth that it was possible to address using cognitive restructuring. She was able to make connections between these thoughts and feelings and past events.

Helen aged 16 had required a period of in-patient treatment for anorexia nervosa and depression. While she was an in-patient she had been able to disclose that she had been raped by youths in her community at the age of 12 and had been unable to tell anyone fearing that she would not be believed and that her parents would be angry. Helen's symptoms of depression and her self-induced weight loss responded to in-patient treatment programmes and when her weight had normalised she was keen to be discharged. Helen began CBT prior to discharge and this was continued as an out-patient.

At this time Helen experienced symptoms of anxiety, sleep disturbance, headaches, fear of boys, episodic low moods and flashbacks of her experiences. Helen was an only child and her mum suffered from multiple sclerosis and her father had struggled to manage, himself becoming quite depressed. Family therapy had been helpful and in the context of family meetings Helen had told her parents about what had happened to her. Helen was keen to develop strategies for managing her moods and improve her confidence and self-esteem. She attended appointments with her mother or alone and was motivated to work and compliant with homework exercises.

Initially in CBT Helen and the clinician developed a shared formulation of how her experience of being raped had impacted on her thinking about herself and her world. She described negative critical thoughts about herself that she was responsible for the assault. This led to understanding the links between her negative automatic thoughts, underlying beliefs and mood states and symptoms of anxiety. Some psychoeducation work around physical symptoms of anxiety and relaxation techniques was useful. Helen appreciated that her mood had lifted over the course of her in-patient treatment and had found antidepressants useful. Her suicidal thinking had reduced and she was able to feel hopeful that she could 'move on'. Helen did not want to talk about her experiences and chose to use distraction techniques and externalision to manage her flashbacks. She was able to 'encapsulate' the flashbacks using visual imagery techniques and choose not to engage with them. The frequency of her flashbacks reduced from ten per day to one or two per week. Using personalised diaries Helen recorded her moods and switches in mood enabling greater understanding of triggers. She worked hard to develop strategies for managing difficult situations and how to protect herself. Helen's confidence improved gradually as she started to attend college and resume contact with her friends.

This case illustrates that symptoms of depression co-occur with anorexia nervosa and PTSD. Helen displayed multiple risk-taking behaviours and the underlying aetiology was an abusive experience in the setting of difficult family relationships at a formative time in her development. Helen required a period of in-patient treatment to manage risk of starvation and of completed suicide. CBT is useful at many levels. For Helen, when her acute symptoms had begun to resolve CBT was a very useful intervention in her on-going recovery. At this stage she was motivated and able to work collaboratively. At an earlier stage this was not possible.

Suicidality

Self-harming behaviour often reflects complex underlying difficulties and may be associated with severe psychiatric disorders including as a symptom of depression, post traumatic stress disorder, conduct disorder or psychosis. Self-harm may reflect suicidality or may be a coping mechanism. A detailed assessment of the range of behaviours, an understanding of suicidal intent and a diagnostic formulation is essential prior to offering a treatment plan including risk management. This has been discussed in brief in Chapter 3.

Definition of self-harm

The definition of suicidal behaviour varies widely among researchers and clinicians. Some use a broad definition and include accident-proneness and unnecessary risk-taking, others use narrow criteria and only include intentional behaviours that lead to immediate death or serious self-injury. NICE Guidance (2004) defined self-harm as 'an expression of personal distress usually made in private by an individual who hurts him/herself. The nature and meaning of the self-harm vary greatly from person to person. The reason a person harms him/herself may be different on each occasion and should not be presumed to be the same.'

Methods of self-harm can be divided into two broad groups: self-injury and self-poisoning.

- Self-injury: cutting, swallowing objects, insertion of objects into the body, burning, hanging, stabbing, shooting, jumping from heights or into vehicles.

- Self-poisoning: overdosing with medicines, swallowing poisonous substances.

- Other risk-taking behaviours: smoking, alcohol, recreational drugs, substance misuse, over-eating, food restriction, promiscuity.

The concept of a continuum of suicidal behaviours from ideation to attempts to completion is generally recognised. In clinical practice, ideators, attempters and completers are distinct but overlapping groups. A past history of suicide attempts represents the strongest known predictor for future suicide attempts and completion. Although not all completers have a history of attempt, approximately one-third of suicide completers have made a previous attempt. Among suicide attempters, it has been estimated that from 0.1% to 10% will eventually kill themselves. Repeated self-harm is a risk factor for completed suicide.

Adolescent suicide is increasing in occurrence especially in young men (Shaffer and Piacentini, 1994). Self-poisoning is the commonest reason for hospital admission in young women (Hawton and Fagg, 1992). Repetition rates are about 10% and are strongly associated with psychological disorder such as depression (Taylor and Stansfield, 1984). Around a third of adolescents who kill themselves have made previous attempts.

As there is a strong association between suicide attempts and depression the cognitive clinician needs to be aware of the implications. Suicidal ideation is common. It is important to fully assess risk. Carr (2002b) stressed the importance of using formulations to specify predisposing and triggering factors that led to an escalation from suicidal ideation to intention or suicidal intention to self. Some factors present a higher risk so are particularly important in assessment.

High risk factors for suicide

- Previous attempts of suicide.
- Medically serious self-harm.
- Substance misuse.
- Chronic pain.
- Mental illness especially depression.
- Antisocial personality disorder or impulsive and aggressive behaviour.
- Wanting to die (strong intention).
- Hopelessness and lack of hope for future.
- Poor supervision.
- Precautions taken against being found.
- Planned – the more time, effort and detail the more worrying.
- Meant as final act.
- Experience of sexual or physical abuse.
- Major loss or life event.
- No attempt to gain help.
- Dangerous method.

Risk assessment

Assessing risk is a continuous process that needs to take place over time and in different settings. It is important to interview parents and the young person separately and together. Asking about the suicide attempt or ideation does not increase the risk. It is important to know if the young person intended to die. Behaviours presenting low medical risk, for instance ingestion of drugs at well below lethal doses may reflect lack of knowledge not absence of intent to die. Similarly the level of planning involved is another indicator of suicidal intention. If, for instance, the young person had planned an attempt when no one was around, collected tablets for a long time, organised their belongings and left a suicide note, it is of very serious concern. However, an impulsive act also may carry a risk of accidental death. The chosen method of self-harm is important. Boys tend to pick more violent methods for instance, hanging, jumping off a bridge. Girls are more likely to overdose, which may present a greater likelihood of life-saving intervention. Substance misuse, drugs and alcohol, are also risk factors.

Some factors are likely to increase hopelessness, a symptom of depression associated with suicidal ideation. These can be life events that involve stress or loss such as a Court appearance, family illness or separation from family. A lack of personal coping skills such as being impulsive, unable to reflect or talk about feelings and to seek support will put a young person more at risk. Effective family communication patterns and a good level of support and supervision can act as protective factors.

A careful clinical formulation should determine young people's mental health, social care and physical care needs and how these should be met. There are issues of confidentiality, safety and supervision involved. The young person will need to understand that when they are at risk their confidentiality will not be maintained and that those responsible for them will need to know. Parents will need to be advised about the level of supervision of the young person that will be required including possibly 24-hour observation in the short term. Availability of means of self-harm in the home will need consideration and appropriate action taken. The clinician will need to make a judgement of the parents' understanding of risk and their ability to implement the required action. Discussion of the circumstances and presentation of the young person will be discussed with a senior colleague as a matter of good practice. The service will be likely to have frequent reviews while risk remains of major concern.

For those who are clinically depressed and at immediate high risk of suicide in-patient care may be indicated and a referral to an in-patient adolescent psychiatric service made.

For a review of therapeutic interventions and evidence see Hawton and Rodham (2006). There is accumulating evidence that CBT can be effective in reducing repetition of self-harm. In the Treatment for Adolescents with Depression Study (TADS) (TADS, 2004) depressed adolescents aged between 12 and 17 years were allocated randomly to receive one of four treatments each lasting 12 weeks (fluoxetine alone, CBT alone, CBT with fluoxetine, placebo). Most favourable outcomes occurred for CBT with fluoxetine. Both groups including CBT showed the greatest reduction in suicidality.

- Self-harming behaviour may indicate risk of completed suicide and should always receive a careful and sensitive assessment.
- If risk of suicide is low, a treatment programme can be discussed of which CBT will be an important component.
- It is good practice to discuss risk assessment of suicidality with a senior colleague.
- The presence of a safe environment is essential before treatment commences.
- Continuing assessment of suicidal risk is important in treatment of depression.

CBT and suicidality

Young people engaged in CBT for depression will be at high risk of suicidality and self-harming behaviour. It is important that a non-judgemental and supportive approach is taken by the clinician and that appropriate goals are set by the young person in managing these problems. Self-harming behaviours commonly encountered within CBT include self-cutting, burning, hitting, excessive use of drugs and alcohol, risk and promiscuity. Chaotic eating patterns including bingeing and vomiting are also common. Suicidal thinking and urges need to be identified and incorporated into a risk management structure.

If the initial presentation to mental health services has been an act of self-harm, following assessment it will be important to determine key problems as the young person sees them. Risk assessments will continue to play a part in sessions and it will be important to agree reviews of treatment and progress and contingencies for a deterioration in the clinical situation.

In CBT the clinician may be able to make a 'no self-harm' contract with the young person and agree to be involved in a set number of sessions. The carers or parents may need to agree to provide 24-hour supervision. Once the acute risks have diminished, treatment for any underlying depression can continue although it is important to continue to monitor suicidal ideation.

Self-harm or suicidal behaviour can be included in a formulation of the young person's difficulties. For many young people self-harm is seen as a coping mechanism and they can be interested and engaged in therapy on the basis of developing alternative strategies. Suicidal behaviour clearly needs to be managed within a safe environment with close working with parents or carers. The formulation will include other depressive symptoms and an analysis of the underlying beliefs and assumptions and negative automatic thoughts and styles of thinking that maintain them.

Strategies used commonly in CBT in the management of suicidality and deliberate self-harm include distraction from thoughts of self-harm and developing alternative ways of managing overwhelming emotion (see Chapter 6). Suicidal content may emerge in challenging negative automatic thoughts, cognitive distortions and core beliefs. Work with parents may include techniques for 'grounding' that is parents being aware of and responding to a need for greater supervision.

- Continuous risk assessment and management is essential in therapeutic work.
- Engaging young people in sharing an understanding of their self-harming behaviour is crucial.
- Distraction and emotional first aid can be helpful.
- Young people who act on suicidal urges will need therapy within safe containing environments.
- Risk assessment should also identify protective factors and agree crisis strategies.

Emerging borderline personality disorder in adolescents

Personality disorder refers to a pattern of inner experiences and behaviour that deviates markedly from the expectations of an individual's culture, is pervasive and inflexible, has an onset in adolescence, is stable over time and leads to distress and impairment (DSM-IV, American Psychiatric Association, 1994). Core features of borderline or emotionally unstable personality disorder (ICD-10, WHO, 1993) are emotional instability, interpersonal instability, identity disturbance, impulsivity and frantic attempts to avoid real and imagined abandonment. Features of most personality disorders can be recognised in adolescence and diagnosis can be made under 18 years using adult criteria for all but antisocial personality disorder which can only be diagnosed over 18 years.

Young people presenting to child and adolescent mental health services (CAMHS) with depressive disorders are a heterogeneous group. Some young people may be 'resistant' to using CBT or its benefits. Core features suggestive of an emerging borderline personality disorder may be recognised. A degree of emotional instability, interpersonal instability and identity confusion are normal during adolescence therefore pervasiveness and persistence of symptoms and considerable caution is applied in making a diagnosis. The term 'emerging personality disorder' is clinically useful in referring to young people under the age of 18 presenting with some features resulting in impairment where adult criteria may not be met. The NICE Guidance (2009) recognises the use of qualifying terms and recommends that it is unlikely that the diagnosis will be made before the age of 16 or 17 years.

Features suggestive of an emerging personality disorder that may be recognised during CBT include the following:

- dependency on individual therapist time and resistance to discharge
- emotional instability rather than pervasive low mood. Self-monitoring and affective education are very useful
- young person resists involvement of family/carers
- chronic 'emptiness' rather than depressed mood
- self-harm as a means of managing intense emotion
- interpersonal difficulties featuring excessive sensitivity and not responsive to social problem-solving
- identity disturbance
- repeated crises precipitated by threat of rejection/loss.

Experience of child sexual, physical and emotional abuse, disruption of primary caring relationships and family history of mental health and personality disorder are risk factors for young people in developing personality disorders in adulthood.

CBT can be a very useful intervention for young people presenting with features described above although the level of complexity is likely to require long-term involvement. Managing problems in CBT is further discussed in Chapter 11.

> For some young people with complex difficulties, depression may be related to wider problems in personality and social relationships. Challenges in therapy may arise that indicate that the young person may have an emerging personality disorder. CBT techniques can provide a structured, helpful intervention but the pacing of therapy may need review.

11

Common problems

Evidence has been presented in Chapter 2 for the efficacy of cognitive behaviour therapy (CBT) in treatment of depression in young people. CBT will however not be effective in all cases and clinicians are likely to experience a range of difficulties. Young people also describe problems in their experience of this form of therapy. Treatment failures are likely to be instructive for clinicians. 'Resistance' to treatment is complex and multi-factorial. This chapter gives an overview of common problems encountered in CBT which can, if not addressed contribute to treatment failure.

Common problems described by clinicians

- Non-attendance.
- Young person does not feel better.
- Young person does not speak.
- Young person does not complete homework.
- Young person does not have thoughts.
- Frequent crises mean that therapy sessions are disrupted.
- Young person getting worse including an increase in risky behaviours, suicidality.
- Refusal to involve parents.
- Dependency.
- Crying throughout session.
- Developing more symptoms.

> **Common problems described by young people or their parents or carers**
>
> - Makes me feel worse.
> - Don't like home practice.
> - Not helping.
> - Don't feel understood.
> - Can't keep taking time off school/work.
> - I don't want my parents involved.
> - Don't know what we can do (parents).

Most problems fall in to one or more of the following three areas.

Environmental/systemic problems

A young person's living situation may be characterised by insurmountable adversity such as chronically ill parents, significant loss events, psycho-social disadvantage and impairment in their quality of life that is core to their presenting psychological problems. These life situations may result in the young person being 'unsafe'. An alternative environment may be required in order that they can access treatment. Environmental adversity may also limit the young person's attending appointments and putting into practice CBT techniques and strategies. If young people with very significant adversity engage in CBT, it may be that their negative thoughts appear realistic rather than abnormal. Parents experiencing adversity may be so overwhelmed with their problems that they may not be psychologically or practically available to their children.

Solutions to these problems are in addressing environmental adversity outside of CBT. This may involve considering social care interventions, alternative educational environments, hospital admissions and identifying separate support for parents and carers. The CBT clinician will often be working within a care team. Partnership working and coordination of care will be very important.

Mismatch between CBT and young person

The initial assessment will have considered suitability for CBT (see Chapter 3). The initial sessions of CBT provide an opportunity for on-going assessment and re-formulation. Symptoms of depression, the adolescents' temperament and capacity for making a therapeutic relationship together with an assessment of their developmental functioning is part of this assessment.

Symptoms of there being a mismatch between CBT and the young person are signs of the young person struggling to engage in CBT or evidence that the young person's depressive symptoms are worsening despite CBT.

Functional deterioration of young people can produce most of the common problems listed. Self-harming or other risky behaviours require regular risk assessment that tends to over-ride therapeutic work.

Non-engagement in CBT can be demonstrated by not attending appointments, not speaking, non-cooperation generally, not doing homework and hostility towards the clinician. For any of these problems re-assessment is indicated. A silent young person may be severely depressed with psychomotor retardation and profound hopelessness. Hostility and anger may reflect relationships and agendas outside of CBT that could be very usefully addressed. A young person may be very anxious and lacking in confidence so that 1:1 sessions may be overwhelming and distressing. Some young people find individual verbal approaches too difficult.

If any of the above are occurring in CBT, re-assessment or re-appraisal is indicated. This may result in a trial of antidepressant medication, additional support for parents or re-formulating the goals of therapy. It is helpful to have a review session with parents and other professionals involved after 4–6 sessions of CBT. If progress is not being made and the young person is not able to engage, this can be discussed constructively. Within this forum it may be agreed that the young person cannot use CBT currently.

Mismatch between CBT clinician and young person

There is an appreciation that clinician experience and expertise is related to young person outcome. Transference and countertransference are terms utilised in psychodynamic therapies to refer to the therapeutic relationship. Adolescents frequently relate differently with different professionals. Some young people avoid relationships and fear trust, others tend to become over dependent. These issues are influenced by the young persons' experience of attachment and parental relationships. Although in CBT the emphasis is on the techniques used in sessions, a relationship where young people are empowered to manage their difficulties and work collaboratively on identified goals is crucial. Some adolescents are not able to engage in this way. Clinician skills in interpreting and managing problems in therapy are important. CBT supervision is essential in order to develop and maintain an effective therapeutic relationship.

Young people may behave in ways that interfere with their receiving CBT and therefore fail to make progress. These behaviours may include not attending sessions, not paying attention in sessions, or not complying with CBT. It is also important to recognise that clinicians may also behave in ways that interfere with the young person receiving CBT. These include cancellation of appointments, lateness, forgetfulness, allowing interruptions in sessions, judgemental attitudes, inconsistency and breaches of confidentiality.

Young people feeling 'not helped' or 'confused' together with evidence of disengagement or non-engagement would be common signs of problems within the therapeutic relationship. An opportunity to discuss these issues with the young person and their carer possibly involving the clinical supervisor may be very helpful in understanding the problems and addressing them. It is important not to agree to an alternative clinician before any disruption in the therapeutic relationship has been carefully considered. It can be therapeutic to work through these issues in CBT by re-formulating the young persons' primary difficulties and changing the goals of therapy.

Problem analysis and solutions

The solution to the majority of problems is re-assessment and review with the young person and family to work out a solution or a way forward.

The importance of psycho-education cannot be underestimated (see Chapter 3). Young people understanding the rationale for therapeutic techniques and strategies is important in helping them to try them. Throughout this book presenting the rationale for therapy to young people has been described and this may need to be repeated or modified according to young persons' ability and developmental stage.

Motivation for change tends to fluctuate and is complex. An aspect of clinician re-appraisal may include assessment of the young person's motivational stage together with using a motivational enhancement approach with young persons in helping them to interpret and work with problems encountered. The model of motivational interviewing was described in Chapter 4.

> It is important to give effective psycho-education at the start of therapy. Strategies to reduce problems include regular re-assessment and review and collaborative working.

In summary, CBT with any young person is a therapeutic journey. Problems or setbacks are inevitable and provide opportunities for learning and ultimately progress.

Throughout this book techniques and strategies used in CBT have been described. These need to be modified according to individual young person need and may or may not be effective. A cognitive formulation is an opportunity for the CBT clinician to identify the strengths and weaknesses that each young person brings to CBT.

In principle any problem needs to be understood by the young person and clinician in a collaborative way in keeping with the CBT relationship. CBT supervision is essential. Most problems can be worked through and with periodic reviews CBT can continue.

Materials and worksheets

Materials and worksheets

1 Clinician prompt sheets

Clinician prompt sheet: engagement and goal setting

Aims

1 To obtain an understanding of the young person's current difficulties.
2 To identify areas of strength.
3 To define goals of therapy.

Tasks

1 Introduction of therapy

Acknowledge appreciation for the young person's participation.

Why are they there? Find out the young person's reasons for attendance and objectives for the therapy.

Set meeting days and times, and discuss how long the therapy is likely to take.

Explain about confidentiality.

Young people's handouts on CBT and on depression

2 Assessment of current difficulties

The goal is to get an overall picture of the present situation as the young person sees it. This involves pinpointing major problems, and gathering enough information to make a preliminary formulation.

Use the information already gathered, keeping in mind the following areas:

- symptoms e.g. sleep problems, worries, or other anxiety symptoms
- life problems e.g. contact with parents, educational problems
- interpersonal and social problems e.g. problems with friends
- associated negative thoughts e.g. 'nothing will change'
- onset/context of depression — 'was there a time when you felt OK?'
- hopelessness/suicidal thoughts — 'does life feel worth living?'

3 Drawing up a problem list

Draw up a list of problems identified by the young person. Help them to rate the severity of each problem using for instance a 1–10 scale.

4 Goal definition

Goals in relation to each problem area are then identified and recorded. Goals must be realistic and clearly defined so that it is clear when they are achieved; for example, 'How would you know if you were getting on better with your Mum?' Asking the young person to write down goals for themselves encourages ownership.

5 Summary of therapy

The young person is given information about practical matters such as number, duration of frequency of session, use of home practice and arrangements for making contact in case of need. The core principles of therapy can be repeated.

Clinician prompt sheet: emotional recognition

Aims

1 To clarify meaning of different emotions e.g. anger, sadness.
2 To help the young person distinguish between different emotional states and between feelings and thoughts.
3 To help the young person observe their own and other people's emotions.
4 To start linking emotions and mood with behaviour and thoughts.

Tasks

Young person uncovers emotional recognition cards, one at a time:

'During the sessions, we will be talking about the way you feel and about ways of helping you feel better in the future; people use different names to describe the way they feel. Therefore, it is important for me to check with you what you call different types of feelings. If you find it difficult to give a definition, you can use an example of how someone might be experiencing this feeling'.

Names of the following emotions can be written on separate coloured cards that are covered and put in front of the young person:

Ashamed   Hurt
Confused/mixed up   Left out
Excited   Lonely
Frustrated   Angry
Guilty   Sad/unhappy
Happy   Scared
                                               Upset

1 They are asked to describe the emotional state: 'How does it feel to be . . .'
2 The young person is asked to give an example of recently feeling like this.
   What were they doing and thinking at the time?
3 The young person is encouraged to make the link between their feelings and behaviour.

Home practice

What was happening/what I was doing	What I was feeling	What I was thinking

Practise by recalling two recent emotional states, for instance feeling happy and feeling sad. If the young person finds it difficult to complete any of the columns, they are encouraged to recall the appropriate mood/event/thought. The young person is asked to recognise when they are angry/sad/anxious/happy and write down what was happening, and what they were doing and thinking at the time.

The young person is reminded that it will be very important to complete the diary and bring it to the next session. Before closing the session, the therapist checks that the young person understood what they are supposed to do.

Clinician prompt sheet: activity scheduling (2 sessions)

Aims

1 To enable the young person to reinforce positive behaviour and gain a sense of control over their life.
2 To enable the young person to make a link about the positive effect of activity on mood.
3 To evaluate the level of boredom and inactivity and its interaction with depressed mood.

Tasks

1 Therapist elicits from the young person which activities they find pleasurable and whether this has changed. If the young person is no longer engaging in these activities the therapist explores possible reasons.
2 Therapist uses an activity diary to fill in examples of a recent day's activities with the young person at a level of detail that is briefly descriptive.

Home practice

Completing a diary for the following week is the homework task. Give handout on activity scheduling (see p. 185)

Following session: activity scheduling

Review diary in detail. Explain concepts of pleasure and achievement as important factors in improving mood.

1 The young person is asked to schedule an activity for each day that could be enjoyable or give a sense of achievement. If an activity for each day seems over-ambitious, the young person and therapist may choose two or three for the week. (Activity is likely to need a parent's permission and support.)
2 The young person can be asked to rate each new activity for pleasure and sense of achievement on 1–10 scales.
3 The young person can be asked to give a self-reward for completing the activity.

   Include parents as appropriate.

Home practice

The young person is asked to continue to keep an activities diary. They should be encourage to achieve at least one targeted activity each day.

Clinician prompt sheet: managing sleep problems

Aims

Take a detailed history.

Tasks

Use a sleep diary (see p. 184).
General strategies:

- bedtime routine
- relaxation, list of calming activities.

    Agree times, process with young person and parent or carer.
    Difficulties settling:

- relaxation tape
- reading or music
- checks from parents.

Night waking:

- personalised strategy for instance read for a fixed period, thought stopping, distraction.

Day–night reversal:

- use sleep diary
- activity schedules
- setting goals.

Clinician prompt sheet: eliciting and recording negative automatic thoughts (NATs)

Aims

1 Detection of automatic thoughts.
2 Recording NATs.
3 Continuing assessment/re-appraisal of functioning and risk.
4 Examine diary from previous week and identify material.

Explaining the rationale to the young person

The young person and therapist will act together as 'scientific collaborators' who will 'investigate' the young person's thinking. The therapist elicits the young person's ideas about the nature of their problems and uses an introduction such as: 'The ways in which we think about things affects our mood. Young people who are depressed often have ways of thinking which mean that they tend to look on the bad side of things. We are going to work together to identify these thoughts and challenge them. This is similar to the work we did at the beginning. Do you remember?'

Techniques

1 Direct questioning. Remind the young person of previous work about difference between feelings and thoughts.
2 Ask about pleasant and unpleasant events and examine diary. Look back through the diary to homework tasks, highlighting 'The thought detective'.
   Check understanding.
   Ask the young person about recent experiences:

   • pleasant event
   • unpleasant event
   • thoughts prior to the appointment.

3 Ask about mental imagery.
   If the young person is unclear the therapist can define a cognition as 'either a thought or a picture in your mind that you may not be aware of unless you focus your attention on it'.

   Promote discussion of associated thoughts. If the young person has difficulty with the terminology, the therapist may use other terms to describe cognitive phenomena such as 'the things you say to yourself' or 'self-statements'.

Clinician prompt sheet: identifying beliefs and thinking errors

Aims

To develop previous work in identifying and recording negative automatic thoughts towards identifying beliefs and assumptions underlying the young person's depressive presentation.

Tasks

1 Use of questioning to elicit beliefs.

- Look for themes in thought records.
- Core beliefs concern oneself, others, the world.
- Take young person's descriptions to a deeper level by asking 'if that were true what would it mean to you?' (downward arrow technique)
- Re-frame statements to challenge the young person's beliefs. For example 'Can you explain how you consistently get top marks for your exams but believe that you are a failure at school?'
- Ask for more clarification 'I'm puzzled that you think that you are disliked yet you went out with friends three times last week?'

2 Identify faulty cognitive styles (use thinking errors fact sheet).

- All or nothing thinking (find a middle way).
- Over-generalisation (judge everything on its own merits).
- Discounting the positives (turning a compliment into an insult).
- Jumping to conclusions (mind reading, fortune telling).
- Magnification/minimisation (looking at the world through binoculars).
- Emotional reasoning (because you feel guilty you think that you have done something wrong).
- Should statements (beating yourself up).
- Labelling (one swallow doesn't make a summer).
- Personalisation (taking things personally).

3 Consider the involvement of family or carers if limited progress made with the young person alone.

Home practice

Completing a thought challenging sheet in the session can be very helpful. Agree diary task. Personalised charts must be salient to the session.

Clinician prompt sheet: challenging negative thinking

Aims
To support the young person in learning to challenge negative thinking.

Tasks

Cognitive restructuring techniques

1 Reality testing
Using information in the young person's diary ask them to find a recent event that they have found difficult.

- Rate believability (out of 100%). For instance: 'I have no friends. 80%'.
- Examine evidence in favour of belief and write one sentence that summarises this. For instance: 'I used to enjoy going out with my friends but since my best friend got a boyfriend, another friend moved away and my sister changed schools I don't go out much.'
- Examine evidence not in support of the thought or belief. For instance, 'My friend still phones me a lot and asks me out. I'm planning to go to stay with my other friend soon.'
- If someone I know was in the situation what would I say to them?
- Create a balanced thought or belief. For instance 'At the moment my friendship group has changed. Various things have happened at once. My friends still care for me but I need to make new friends now'.

2 Design a behavioural experiment
- Operationalise beliefs. 'So how could we test out that that is true?'
- Design a simple experiment and record what happens. If the belief is that 'nothing I do improves my mood' you could use activity sceduling to test if this is true.

3 Challenging thinking styles (see handouts, pp. 188, 189)
- Monitor all or nothing thinking.
- Adopt the middle ground.

4 Repeated re-evaluation
- How much do you believe the thought?
- Remember that thinking negative thoughts in sessions can be difficult.
- Distraction techniques can be used if the young person is so distressed when thoughts arise:

  - focus on an object;   - sensory awareness;   - thought stopping.

Home practice (see handout, p. 190)

The young person is asked to act as a 'thought detective' for the next week. Each day, negative thoughts should be recorded in the diary. The young person is encouraged to weigh up the evidence that supports or rejects them. As cognitive techniques are introduced, diaries which build in cognitive restructuring techniques can be introduced.

Home practice review

Each week young person and therapist review entry to diary.

Clinician prompt sheet: communication and interpersonal skills

Aims

1 To elicit and work on communication difficulties.
2 To improve interpersonal skills.
3 To give the young person the message that the skills can be learnt.
4 To link improvement in social relationships with improved mood.

Communication skills

1 'Getting on well with people involves communication. Do you know what that means? Communication consists of *listening* to others as well as *talking* to others. To have a *conversation* you need to *start* one and be able to *continue* one. Before all of this you need to *get to know* new people. These are the skills which we are going to practise today.'
2 Look at stills on page 112 as a basis, go through the main features of listening and conversation skills.
3 Examples to generate discussion: Ask young person if they are a good listener or if they know someone who is, give examples. Ask for examples of recent conversations with problems. Break these down into the skills above and using role play, if appropriate, practise listening and conversation skills.
4 Share the information about skills of 'introducing myself'. Ask the young person when they last met somebody new, talk about difficulties with making new friends, meeting new people. As with listening and conversation skills, use role play where appropriate.

Interpersonal skills

'The next set of exercises involve working on talking to people and on thinking more about getting on with friends, parents, teachers better.'
   Share the information in the handout and explore difficulties in each area. Use role play as appropriate.

* *Joining in*: explore current difficulties for example feeling left out, lonely.
* *Sharing*: explore difficulties for example with siblings, peers, jealousy, rivalry.
* *Complimenting*: experiences of complimenting others and being understood.

Home practice instructions

The home practice task will depend on the work covered in the session and on the young person's individual difficulties. The young person might be asked to initiate one conversation per day over the coming week and record these in their diary. In addition, the therapist explores the potential for the young person to meet new people, introduce themselves and use other interpersonal skills practised in the session. The young person is asked to pay attention to arguments over the week with parents, peers, teachers and to record these in the diary. The aim is to encourage the young person to monitor and record difficulties with social relationships.

Clinician prompt sheet: social problem-solving

Aims

1 To help the young person clarify specific ways of approaching social and interpersonal problems. It is important to highlight the notion of 'small everyday problems' rather than major crises or life events.
2 To link improvement in social relationships with mood.
3 To combine work on communication and interpersonal skills with interpersonal problem-solving.

Problem-solving

1 Share the handout 'seven steps to solving problems'.
2 Using the previous week's diary choose a problem situation. The young person is asked to clarify which particular aspect of this situation or interaction is most difficult and uses it to brainstorm options.

Examples of difficulties:

Initiating or keeping a conversation going with another young person
Joining in activities with other young people for instance, breaks at school
Asking for something in class or home
Arguments with parents or peers
Handling an argument
Standing up for oneself at school or home

---

3 The young person is asked to choose a social situation in which they encounter difficulties. The young person and therapist then work through the seven steps. Repeat with another problem if felt necessary. The examples may be useful if the young person is unable to think of one.

Home practice

A problem that the young person can work on outside of the session is identified or the young person has identified or the young person can put into action an agreed solution and feedback in the following session.

Clinician prompt sheet: ending therapy

Aims

1 To summarise treatment so far.
2 To review specific links between the initial symptoms and the work in different sessions, which implies that the themes of the therapy could be of further help in the future.
3 To compare the way the young person currently feels with their mood at the beginning of therapy, and recognise how they have tackled these symptoms.
4 To focus on particular aspects of the therapy that they found helpful.
5 To think of specific areas of remaining difficulties, which are yet to be resolved.
6 To help the young person identify how to work on these ideas after the end of therapy.
7 To reinforce the young person's belief in themselves as able to influence how they feel.
8 To identify any possible stresses that might lead to future difficulties, identify 'first signs' and discuss how and when to make contact again.

Tasks

1 General review.

The young person is asked to think back to the beginning of therapy. Specific goals identified can be referred to. Particular importance is paid to the young person's depressed mood at the outset of therapy. Diaries or records can help.

2 Review of the therapy.

The therapist defines and repeats the main themes of the treatment to the young person and links them to the formulation. Discuss what the young person has felt has been helpful. A therapy 'blueprint' may be used to describe what has been discussed.

3 Further actions.

The therapist and young person can also discuss in more detail any remaining difficulties and appropriate actions.

The following *key messages* are given to the young person:

- plans from the service once the therapy sessions have come to an end, if further follow-up is planned
- the young person achieved changes through their own efforts
- if any problems arise, or the feelings of sadness return, or it is difficult to cope be clear about who they can tell, methods of further contact with the therapist or other options for help. Using diaries can be helpful.

2 Materials for use in CBT

CBT model of depression

Early experience

Formation of dysfunctional beliefs

Critical incident

Assumptions activated

Negative automatic thoughts

Symptoms of depression

Behaviour   **Moods**   **Thoughts**   **Physical reactions**

 Materials and worksheets from *Depression* by Chrissie Verduyn, Julia Rogers and Alison Wood published by Routledge

Young person's fact sheet:

What is depression?

Anyone can get depressed. It is the most common psychological problem. It varies from person to person but often stressful and difficult things can trigger depression. We all feel sad from time to time but usually the feeling passes. With depression these feelings of sadness just seem to go on and on.

Main features of depression in teenagers

Depression can affect how you feel, how you think and things that you do.

- Negative styles of thinking may include:

    o low self-esteem/confidence
    o feeling things are hopeless and no one can help
    o feeling inadequate or that everyone else is better than you.

- Difficulties with friends may include:

    o reducing your social activities
    o falling out with people you used to get on with.

- Symptoms of depression may include:

    o feeling sad and crying easily
    o having trouble sleeping
    o becoming less active
    o loss of interest in things you use to enjoy
    o feeling like harming yourself
    o having no motivation and feeling tired most of the time
    o losing your appetite
    o it is hard to concentrate
    o losing your temper more easily
    o feeling guilty.

The problem with depression is that the symptoms can make you feel worse and worse. For instance, if you stop going out then you don't see your friends and it gets harder to be sociable. Depression can make you feel like there is no way out but help starts here.

Young person's fact sheet:

What is CBT?

CBT or cognitive behaviour therapy is a therapy that helps young people get over their depression and the problems related to the depression. There is a great deal of research that shows CBT helps.

A cycle occurs where the depression changes a person's thoughts, feelings and behaviour or TFB.

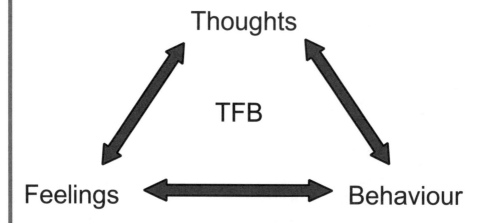

CBT sessions usually last for 6 to 12 weeks. The therapist and the young person work together to understand the problems and set goals. Then the therapist teaches new skills to make things better. When a young person is depressed it changes how they think and process information. CBT focuses on the links between THOUGHTS, FEELINGS and BEHAVIOUR. The aim of the CBT is to change some of the behaviours and thoughts and reduce the symptoms of depression. An important part of the therapy is the home practice where the new skills are practised.

CBT looks at identifying and challenging negative thinking styles. When you are depressed it feels that these thoughts are true but it is the depression. CBT will help you to change your thoughts. Negative styles of thinking can relate to childhood experiences, forming the basis of our beliefs about:

- **self** e.g. 'I am a bad person'
- **others** e.g. 'people can not be trusted'
- **the world** e.g. 'the world is not a safe place'.

CBT will also help to look at problems in relationships and other problems.

Severity rating scale

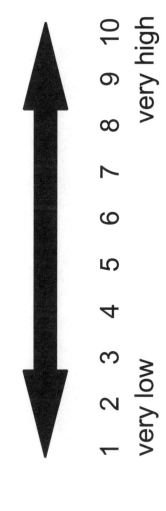

Severity rating scale

1 2 3 4 5 6 7 8 9 10

very low   very high

Mood rating scale

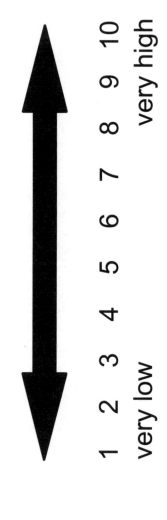

Mood rating scale

1 2 3 4 5 6 7 8 9 10
very low   very high

Materials and worksheets from *Depression* by Chrissie Verduyn, Julia Rogers and Alison Wood published by Routledge

Self-monitoring diary

Pleasant event	Feelings	Thoughts
1		
2		

Unpleasant event	Feelings	Thoughts
1		
2		

Activating yourself fact sheet

The problem

When people feel depressed they tend to slow down both mentally and physically. Everything you do feels like an effort, so you do less, and then you feel bad about doing less. You then start to believe that you can do nothing and that you'll never feel better, or get over it. This makes you feel even more depressed, and it becomes even more difficult to do anything. This is what we call a vicious circle.

The way out

To make you feel better, we need to try and break this vicious circle. A good way to do this is to start by becoming more active.

☆ Activity makes you feel better. If nothing else, activity takes your mind off painful feelings. It can give you the sense of being more in control, and you may even find there are things you enjoy doing.
☆ Activity makes you feel less tired. Normally, when you are tired you need to rest. When you feel depressed, the opposite is true, and you need to do more. Doing nothing will only make you feel even more tired than you feel already.
☆ Activity makes you feel like doing more.
☆ Activity improves your ability to think. This means that putting problems into perspective will become easier.

Becoming more active will help you begin to overcome your depression, but getting started is not always easy. This is because when people are depressed they tend to think negatively of themselves, the world and the future, and therefore tend to find themselves thinking, 'I won't enjoy it', 'I'll only make a mess of it', 'It's too difficult', etc. These thoughts will make taking action even harder. It is important to start with small steps.

Later we will work directly on the thoughts that are stopping you from getting down to what you want to do. We will learn to notice and challenge them, so that they don't stand in your way.

Many depressed people firmly believe that they are doing nothing, achieving nothing, and enjoying nothing. A way to help you plan your day productively and enjoyably is to use an activity schedule. An activity schedule is an hour by hour record of what you do, and is a way of showing just how you are spending your time.

Self-monitoring

1   For the next few days, record exactly what you do, hour by hour.

2   Give each activity a rating of between 1 and 10 for PLEASURE (P) and for ACHIEVEMENT (A). Your pleasure score is how much you enjoyed doing the activity, and your achievement score is how well you thought you did the activity. You can use any number between 1 and 10 to indicate the degree of enjoyment or pleasure you experienced, and the sense of achievement you got from doing it. 10 is the most positive.

3   It is important to rate your activities for P and A when you have just completed the activity, not some time later. If you wait until later your negative thoughts and depressed feelings will make you devalue what you had done earlier. It is much easier to remember things that we don't like or enjoy than the good and positive things we do. Rating your activities immediately will help you to start to notice even small degrees of pleasure and achievement which might have gone unnoticed before.

4   Achievement should be rated according to how difficult the activity was for you now not how difficult it was for you before you got depressed, or how difficult everyone else would find it. When people feel depressed, things that used to be very easy, become difficult, so make sure you give yourself credit when you achieve them.

Your activity schedule will show you in detail exactly what you are doing and enjoying, which will help you to challenge the belief that nothing goes well for you. You may find that you are more active, achieving more, and getting more enjoyment out of things than you had thought. Even if this is not the case, your activity schedule will help you identify what it is that is getting in the way.

Planning ahead

Now that you know how you are spending your time, the next step is to plan each day in advance. You can plan to do the sort of activity that you enjoy and that makes you feel you are achieving something for each day.

1   Planning your time will allow you to feel that you are taking control of your life again, and give you a sense of purpose.

2   Having a set plan for your day will help you to keep focused and will also help you to keep going when you are feeling bad.

3   Once you have set out your day in writing it will seem more manageable. You will have your day broken down into manageable units rather than a long stretch of time that can sometimes feel like forever.

Hints to help you stick to your activity schedule

1   Set aside a particular time each evening to read over what you have done during the day and to plan for tomorrow. It is useful to do this at a time when you are not likely to be interrupted.

2 If you are finding it hard to get down to doing a particular task, for example, doing your homework, tell your muscles in detail what to do. Use specific instructions like 'Sit at desk', 'Pick up book', 'Now read'. As soon as you have told yourself what to do, do it. Don't allow any pause for doubts to creep in.

3 To help get yourself moving remove distractions, such as by turning the television off.

4 Avoid going to bed. Use your bed for sleeping in at night, and not for using during the day. If you feel you need to relax during the day, then do it some other way such as listening to music or reading.

5 Reward yourself for what you have done. For example, you could tell yourself that when you've completed an activity you will have a cup of coffee, a bar of chocolate, or watch TV with your Mum.

6 Give yourself cues for action. You could set an alarm to signal the time to start or end an activity. Put signs up around the house to remind you of what you are supposed to be doing. You could tell someone in your family that say 7:30 is your time for planning the next day, and get them to remind you if you get distracted.

7 Give yourself encouragement. Start the day with an activity that will give you a sense of achievement and that you have a good chance of completing successfully.

8 Try to fill your day with an equal number of things that you enjoy doing and things that give you a sense of achievement.

9 Stick to the pattern of activities that you have found most rewarding and fulfilling in the past, there's a good chance that once you get going you will enjoy it again.

10 Watch out for negative thoughts that tell you you can't do things. Write them down and answer them at once, then act on the answers.

 Materials and worksheets from *Depression* by Chrissie Verduyn, Julia Rogers and Alison Wood published by Routledge

Activity schedule

Name: ....

Week Beginning: ....

Time	Monday	Tuesday	Wednesday	Thursday	Friday	Saturday	Sunday
8–9							
9–10							
10–11							
11–12							
12–1							
1–2							
2–3							
3–4							
4–5							
5–6							
6–7							
7–8							
8–9							
9–10							

Your activity diary

Each day write down what you have been doing and give a score out of 10 for how much you enjoyed it or felt that you had achieved something by doing it.

1 out of 10 means that you didn't enjoy it or feel that you had achieved anything at all by doing it.

10 out of 10 means that you really enjoyed it or felt that you had achieved something by doing it.

Day	Monday	Tuesday	Wednesday	Thursday	Friday	Saturday	Sunday
Morning							
Afternoon							
Evening							

 Materials and worksheets from *Depression* by Chrissie Verduyn, Julia Rogers and Alison Wood published by Routledge

List of rewards

Complete this list on your own or with a parent or friend.

People

Name 2 people that you would like to see more of

1
2

Things

Write down two things that you would really like to have (make sure that they are things such as a magazine or CD that you might afford).

1
2

What are your favourite things to eat?

1
2

What are your favourite drinks (non-alcoholic)?

1
2

What activities have you enjoyed in the past?

1
2

What places have you enjoyed going to in the past?

1
2

Are there other things that you would like to do, have or see that you haven't written above above?

1
2
3
4

I am going to reward myself for:

....

....

....

....

SLEEP DIARY

(−2 = bad/poor; +2 = good)

Name: _____

Fill in date under each day

Remember to complete this diary each morning approximately 15–20 minutes after awakening

	YESTERDAY					THIS MORNING				
	Went to sleep last night, felt (circle one)	Went to bed at: (time)	Fell asleep in: (minutes)	During the night awoke at: (time)	And stayed awake for: (minutes)	During the night awoke at: (time)	Slept a total of: (hours)	When got up this morning felt: (circle one)	Overall, sleep last night was: (circle one)	Use an alarm (yes/no)
Monday	−2 −1 0 +1 +2							−2 −1 0 +1 +2	−2 −1 0 +1 +2	
Tuesday	−2 −1 0 +1 +2							−2 −1 0 +1 +2	−2 −1 0 +1 +2	
Wednesday	−2 −1 0 +1 +2							−2 −1 0 +1 +2	−2 −1 0 +1 +2	
Thursday	−2 −1 0 +1 +2							−2 −1 0 +1 +2	−2 −1 0 +1 +2	
Friday	−2 −1 0 +1 +2							−2 −1 0 +1 +2	−2 −1 0 +1 +2	
Saturday	−2 −1 0 +1 +2							−2 −1 0 +1 +2	−2 −1 0 +1 +2	
Sunday	−2 −1 0 +1 +2							−2 −1 0 +1 +2	−2 −1 0 +1 +2	

Materials and worksheets from *Depression* by Chrissie Verduyn, Julia Rogers and Alison Wood published by Routledge

Negative automatic thoughts (NATs) fact sheet

What are NATs?

We all have lots of thoughts that go through out minds everyday. When people get depressed however, some of these thoughts can be unhelpful and make them feel bad.

We call these types of thoughts negative automatic thoughts, or **NATs**.

It is really important to be able to spot **NATs** so that they can be challenged.

NATs are:

AUTOMATIC – they just come into your mind without any effort. Unless you are looking out for them you might not realise that they're there. **NATs** come when they want to, without giving you a choice, and they can be difficult to stop. It takes lots of practice.

TWISTED – **NATs** present themselves as facts but if you examine them closely, you will usually find that there is little or no evidence for them. They have built themselves on scraps of evidence. This is good because it means they aren't as strong as they might at first seem.

BELIEVABLE – to you that is . . . **NATs** are smart but sneaky. They make sure that you accept them without question. Other people might question them but the **NATs** have brainwashed you into believing whatever they say.

UNHELPFUL – they get you feeling down and then they keep you there. They make it difficult to change.

Here are some examples of **negative automatic thoughts:**

- bad things are always my fault
- everyone thinks I'm boring
- I'll never have any friends
- I'm a failure
- I'm bad
- I'm going to get this wrong
- I'm stupid
- I'm ugly
- my problems will never go away
- no one cares what happens to me
- nobody likes me
- nothing will ever work out for me
- there is nothing to look forward to
- I always have bad luck
- I can't do anything right.

It's important to remember that these sorts of thoughts can seem true when you are depressed, but in reality, they are not true, and you can learn how to change them.

Thinking errors fact sheet

Thinking errors are unhelpful ways of thinking that make you feel bad. We all make these errors from time to time. It only becomes a problem when they happen regularly and stop you from making real choices about what you can and can't do.

There are five main thinking errors to look out for.

1 All or nothing thinking.

This is when you see everything in terms of extremes. Things are either brilliant or terrible, a total success or a complete failure.

For example: Jack made a small mistake and didn't get top marks for his assignment. He thought 'my work is rubbish; I might just as well have failed'. This is an example of all or nothing thinking.

2 Jumping to conclusions.

This can happen in two ways:

Mind reading. Thinking that you know what someone else is thinking or feeling.

For example: Mandy and Tanya were friends. Then Mandy walked past Tanya at school and didn't say hello. Tanya thought 'She ignored me because she doesn't like me. She thinks I'm boring'.

Tanya was mind reading. She guessed that Mandy didn't speak to her because she doesn't like her, rather than thinking that perhaps Mandy didn't see her. She might have been in a rush or had something on her mind.

Predicting the worst. Expecting things to turn out bad.

For example: Ben decided not to go to his geography exam because he thought it would be too hard and he wouldn't be able to answer any of the questions.

Ben was predicting the worst. His thinking error did not fit the facts. He had done lots of revision for the geography exam and so there was no reason why he shouldn't have been able to answer at least some of these questions.

3 Over-generalising or catastrophising

This is thinking that because one thing has gone wrong, everything's going to go wrong and nothing will ever work out well for you.

For example: Stuart had an argument with his dad. He thought 'Dad doesn't understand me, no one understands me or cares about me and they never will'.

4 Shoulds, musts and oughts

This is giving yourself a hard time by using ultimatum words like should, must and ought: 'I should be getting better quicker than this; I must try harder; I ought to have known better'. These sorts of thoughts are likely to make you feel guilty and angry all the time.

5 Blaming yourself

This is feeling responsible for things that aren't your fault.

For example: Sarah's parents were always arguing. She thought 'Mum and Dad keep arguing because I do things that annoy them and put them in a bad mood'.

Mood diary

Please give a rating out of 10 for your feelings and thoughts. The stronger the feeling or thought the higher the rating.

The event or situation What was happening or what was I doing?	Feelings How was I feeling? (1–10)	Thoughts What was I thinking? (1–10)	Feelings after thought challenging Copy the feelings from column two into this column and rate them again (1–10)	Thoughts after thought challenging Copy the thoughts from column three into this column and rate them again (1–10)

Thought challenging worksheet

The NAT that I am going to challenge:

Question 1

What is the evidence for this NAT:

What is the evidence against this NAT:

Question 2

What is an alternative, more balanced thought?

Question 3

Am I making any thinking errors?

- all or nothing thinking
- jumping to conclusions: mind reading or predicting the worst
- over-generalising or catastrophising
- shoulds, musts and oughts
- blaming yourself.

Problem-solving handout

We all have choices of how we behave towards other people. The responses we choose can produce different outcomes. We can therefore think of ourselves as Detectives trying to solve social problems – just as police detectives try to solve crimes.

Step 1: **DETECT**
Stop and think!
    What is the problem?

Step 2: **INVESTIGATE**
What could you do? (think of three different things. Don't worry whether they are the right choices or not.)
    What would happen next? (think of good things and bad.)
    Which of these would be best?

Step 3: **SOLVE**
What are you going to say or do?
    What do you have to remember?

Seven steps to solving problems

1   Define the problem.
        What exactly is the problem? Make it fit into '. . . the problem is how to . . .'
2   Brainstorm to generate possible solutions.
        Think of as many ways you can of solving this problem.
3   Focus energy and attention on the task.
        *Be determined to solve this problem – don't let it beat you. Be sure of why it is
    important to solve the problem.*
4   Project the outcome of each of the possible solutions.
        *What would be the advantages and disadvantages of doing each of the
    things you outlined in Step 2?*
5   Weigh the consequences and choose a solution.
        *Step 4 can take some time! Weigh up the pros and cons and choose a
    solution to try for starters.*
6   Evaluate the outcome of the chosen action.
        See what happens!
7   Give yourself a reward for success or try one of the other possible solutions.
    *If you got it right the first time, well done! Give yourself a treat. If not, don't be too
    disappointed – work your way through your list and try another solution or go
    back to the start and re-define the problem.*

Problem-solving worksheet

What is the problem?

....

....

What could you do? (Think of three different things. Don't worry whether they are the right choices or not.)

1 ....

....

2 ....

....

3 ....

....

What would happen next?

1 ....

....

2 ....

....

3 ....

....

Which of these would be best?

....

....

Make a plan

What are you going to say or do?

....

What do you have to remember?

....

....

Why not have a go? How did you get on?

....

....

Social problem-solving predicaments

A teacher accuses you of doing something serious, like stealing or breaking something in the school. You didn't do it, but you know that one of your mates did. What would you say or do?

Your teacher puts you in detention for something you feel you didn't do. You feel that the teacher is picking on you. What would you say or do?

Somebody in your class opens their desk and you see in it a number of things that have been lost by your friends. What would you say or do? To your friends? To this person?

Your teacher gave you a detention, which you didn't go to. The next day your teacher asks you to wait for him after the lesson. What would you say or do?

You are starting a new school. Nobody seems to want to go round with you or make friends. What would you do or say?

You are starting a new school. Some of the people there start teasing you and calling you names. What would you do or say?

Your younger brother tells you that he is being bullied by some kids in your year. What would you say or do?

One of your school mates tells you that someone at school has been spreading lies about you. What would you do or say? To this mate? To the person who's supposed to have been spreading lies?

Your parents have gone away for the weekend leaving you in charge of the house. Your mates find out and suggest having a party. Your little brother has threatened to tell your parents if anything happens. What would you do?

You are going home from a party. It is after midnight, raining and you are 5 miles away from home. You are worried about getting home late. You are with three of your mates – one of them suggests nicking a car. What would you do?

Your mate had two tickets for a concert. You talked him into giving you one, which was meant for another of his mates. You meet the person the ticket was bought for. What would you do?

You hear from a mate that your boy/girlfriend has been seen with a mate of yours at a party. What would you do?

At work your boss makes a fool of you in front of six of your workmates about dropping and breaking something. You feel embarrassed and angry. What would you do?

Your mum wants you to baby-sit for your little sister on Saturday night but you want to go out. What do you do?

A friend tells you that a girl/boy fancies you. You meet him/her in the street. What do you do?

Someone has been spreading lies about you. What do you do?

You lend a friend your favourite CD. He/she later says that they have lost it. What do you do?

Therapy blueprint

Treatment goals	What helped?

The treatment:

- recognising emotions
- linking events with feelings and thoughts
- rewarding yourself for being able to change
- solving problems in social situations
- checking on thoughts, looking for evidence
- looking for positive causes, consequences, effects on feelings.

References

Achenbach, T.M. (1991) *Manual for the Child Behaviour Checklist/4–18 and 1991 Profile*. Burlington VT: University of Vermont.

Alpert, J.E., Faca, M., Uebelacker, L.A., Nierenberg, A.A., Pava, J.A., Worthington, J.J. and Rosenbaum, J.F. (1999) 'Patterns of Axis I comorbidity in early onset versus late onset major depressive disorder', *Biological Psychiatry* 46, 202–211.

American Psychiatric Association (1980) *Diagnostic and Statistical Manual of Mental and Behavioral Disorders*, 3rd edn (DSM-III). Washington DC: American Psychiatric Association.

American Psychiatric Association (1994) *Diagnostic and Statistical Manual of Mental and Behavioral Disorders*, 4th edn (DSM-IV). Washington DC: American Psychiatric Association.

Andrews, G., Szabo, M. and Burns, J. (2002) 'Preventing major depression in young people, *British Journal of Psychiatry* 181, 460–462.

Andrews, J.A. and Lewinsohn, P.M. (1992) 'Suicidal attempts among older adolescents: prevalence and co-occurrence with psychiatric disorders', *Journal of the American Academy of Child and Adolescent Psychiatry* 31, 655–662.

Angold, A. and Costello, E.J. (1995) The epidemiology of depression in children and adolescents. In Goodyer, I. (ed.) *The Depressed Child and Adolescent*. Cambridge: Cambridge University Press.

Angold, A. and Costello, E.J. (2000) 'The Child and Adolescent Psychiatric Assessment (CAPA)', *Journal of the American Academy of Child and Adolescent Psychiatry* 39, 39–48.

Angold, A., Costello, E.J., and Worthman, C.M. (1998a) 'Puberty and depression, the role of age, pubertal status and pubertal timing', *Psychological Medicine* 28, 51–61.

Angold, A., Messer, S.C., Stangl, D., Farmer, E.M.Z., Costello, E.J. and Burns, B.J. (1998b) 'Perceived parental burden and service use for child and adolescent psychiatric disorders', *American Journal of Public Health* 88, 75–80.

Asarnow, J.R., Goldstein, M.J., Carlson, G.A., Perdue, S., Bates, S. and Keller, J. (1988) 'Childhood-onset depressive disorders. A follow up study of rates of hospitalization and out-of-home placement among child psychiatric inpatients', *Journal of Affective Disorders* 15, 245–253.

Barker, P. (2004) *Basic Child Psychiatry*, 7th edn. London: Blackwell Scientific Publications.

Beck, A. (1990) *Cognitive Therapy of Personality Disorders*. New York: Guilford Press.

Beck, A., Ward, C., Mendelson, M., Mock, J. and Erbaugh, J. (1961) 'An inventory for depression', *Archives of General Psychiatry* 4, 561–571.

Beck, A., Rush, A., Shaw, B. and Emery, G. (1979). *Cognitive Therapy of Depression*. New York: Guilford.

Beck, A., Steer, R.A. and Brown, G.K. (1996) *The Manual for Beck Depression Inventory (BDI–II)*. San Antonio, TX: Harcourt Assessment Inc.

Beck, J.S., Beck, A.T. and Jolly, J.B. (2005) *Youth Depression Inventory*. San Antonio, TX: Harcourt Assessment Inc.

Birleson, P., Hudson, I., Buchanan, D.J. and Wolff, S. (1987) 'Clinical evaluation of a self rating scale for depressive disorder in childhood (Depression Self-Rating Scale)', *Journal of Child Psychology and Psychiatry* 28, 43–60.

Birmaher, B., Brent, D.A. and Benson, R.S. (1998) 'Summary of the practice parameters for the assessment and treatment of children and adolescents with depressive disorders', *Journal of the American Academy of Child and Adolescent Psychiatry* 37, 1237–1238.

Bolton, D., O'Ryan, D., Udwin, O., Boyle, S. and Yule, W. (2000) 'The long term psychological effects of a disaster experienced in adolescence. II General psychopathology', *Journal of Child Psychology and Psychiatry* 41, 513–523.

Brent, D.A., Holden, D., Birmaher, B., Baugher, M., Roth, C., Iyengar, S. and Johnson, B.A. (1997) 'A clinical psychotherapy trial for adolescent depression comparing cognitive, family and supportive therapy', *Archives of General Psychiatry* 54, 877–885.

Carlson, G.A. and Garber, J. (1986) Developmental issues in the classification of depression in children. In Rutter, M., Izard, C. and Read, P. (eds) *Depression in Young People: Developmental and Clinical Perspectives*. New York: Guilford Press.

Carr, A. (2002a) *The Handbook of Child and Adolescent Clinical Psychology. A Contextual Approach* (pp. 911–941). New York: Brunner-Routledge.

Carr, A. (2002b) *Parents, Adolescent and Child Training Skills 2. Depression and Attempted Suicide in Adolescence*. Oxford: Blackwell.

Chen, I.G., Roberts, R.E. and Aday, L.A. (1998) 'Ethnicity and adolescent depression: the case of Chinese Americans', *Journal of Nervous and Mental Disease* 186, 623–630.

Clark, D.M. and Fairburn, C.G. (1997) *The Science and Practice of Cognitive Behaviour Therapy*. Oxford: Oxford University Press.

Clarke, G.N., Lewinsohn, P.M. and Hops, H. (1990) *Instructor's Manual for the Adolescent Coping with Depression Course*. Eugene OR: Castalia Press.

Clarke, G.N., Hornbrook, M., Lynch, F., Polen, M., Gale, J., O'Connor, E., Seeley, J.R. and Debar, L. (2002) 'Group cognitive-behavioural treatment for depressed adolescent offspring of depressed parents in a health maintenance organisation', *Journal of the American Academy of Child and Adolescent Psychiatry* 41, 305–313.

Clarke, G., Debar, L., Lynch, F., Powell, J., Gale, J., O'Connor, E., Ludman, E., Bush, T., Lin, E.H., Von Korff, M. and Hertert, S. (2005) 'A randomized effectiveness trial of brief cognitive behavioural therapy for depressed adolescents receiving antidepressant medication', *Journal of the American Academy of Child and Adolescent Psychiatry* 44, 888–898.

Coopersmith, S. (1967) *The Antecedents of Self Esteem*. San Francisco CA: Freeman.

Coopersmith, S. (1975) *Self Esteem Inventory*. Lafayette CA: Self Esteem Institute.

Corcoran, J. and Franklin, C. (2002) 'Multi-systemic risk factors predicting depression, self-esteem and stress in low SES and culturally diverse adolescents', *Journal of Human Behaviour in the Social Environment* 5, 61–76.

Costello, E.J. and Angold, A. (1988) 'Scales to assess child and adolescent depression: checklists, screens and nets', *Journal of the American Academy of Child and Adolescent Psychiatry* 27, 726–737.

Costello, E.J., Edelbrock, C.S. and Costell, A.J. (1985) 'Validity of the NIMH Diagnostic Interview Schedule for Children: a comparison between psychiatric and paediatric referrals', *Journal of Abnormal Child Psychology* 13, 579–595.

Costello, E.J., Angold, A. and Keeler, G.P. (1999) 'Adolescent outcomes of childhood disorders: the consequences of severity and impairment', *Journal of the American Academy of Child and Adolescent Psychiatry* 38, 121–128.

Coyle, J.T., Pine, D.S., Charney, D.S., Lewis, L., Nemeroff, C.B., Carlson, G.A., Joshi, P.T., Reiss, D., Todd, R.D., Hellander, M.; Depression and Bipolar Support Alliance Consensus Development Panel (2003) 'Depression and bipolar support alliance consensus statement on the unmet needs in diagnosis and treatment of mood disorders in children and adolescents', *Journal of the American Academy of Child and Adolescent Psychiatry* 42, 1494–1503.

Crittenden, P. (2005) *Attachment and Cognitive Psychotherapy (invited address)*. International Congress on Cognitive Psychotherapy, Gotenborg, Sweden, June 2005 (www.patcrittenden.com).

Dalgleish, T., Neshat-Doost, H., Taghavi, R., Moradi, A., Yule, W., Canterbury, R. and Vostanis, P. (1998) 'Information processing in recovered depressed children and adolescents', *Journal of Child Psychology and Psychiatry* 39, 1031–1035.

Deakin, J.F.W. and Crow, T.J. (1986) Monoamines, rewards and punishments; the anatomy of affective disorders. In Deakin, J.F.W. (ed.) *The Biology of Depression* (pp.1–25). London: Royal College of Psychiatrists.

Dietz, L., Birmaher, B., Williamson, D., Silk, J., Dahl, R., Axelson, D., Ehmann, M. and Ryan, N. (2008) 'Mother–child interactions in depressed children and children at high risk and low risk of future depression', *Journal of the American Academy of Child and Adolescent Psychiatry* 47, 574–582.

Doi, V., Roberts, R.E., Takeuchi, K. and Suzuki, S. (2001) 'Multi-ethnic comparison of adolescent major depression based on the DSM-IV criteria in a U.S.-Japan Study', *Journal of the American Academy of Child and Adolescent Psychiatry* 40, 1308–1315.

Donovan, C.L. and Spence, S.H. (2005) Children's interpersonal problems. In Graham, P., *Cognitive Behaviour Therapy for Children and Families*. Cambridge: Cambridge University Press.

Dummett, N. (2006) 'Processes for systemic cognitive behavioural therapy with children young people and families', *Behavioural and Cognitive Psychotherapy* 34, 179–189.

Emslie, G.J., Heiligenstein, J.H., Wagner, K.D., Hoog, S.L., Ernest, D.E., Brown, E., Nilsson, M. and Jacobson, J.G. (2002) 'Fluoxetine for acute treatment of depression in children and adolescents: a placebo controlled randomized clinical trial', *Journal of the American Academy of Child and Adolescent Psychiatry* 41, 1205–1215.

Emslie, G.J., Mayes, T.L., Laptook, R.S. and Batt, M. (2003) 'Predictors of response to treatment in children and adolescents with mood disorders', *Psychiatric Clinics of North America* 26, 435–456.

Fergusson, D.M., Horwood, L.J. and Lynskey, M.T. (1995) 'Maternal depressive symptoms and depressive symptoms in adolescents', *Journal of Child Psychology and Psychiatry* 36, 1161–1178.

Flavell, J. (1967) *The Developmental Psychology of Jean Piaget.* New York: D. Van Nostrand Company.

Fleming, J.E., Offord, D.R. and Boyle, M.H. (1989) 'Prevalence and childhood and adolescent depression in the community Ontario Child Health Study', *British Journal of Psychiatry* 155, 647–654.

Fombonne, E. (1998) 'Interpersonal psychotherapy for adolescent depression', *Clinical Psychology and Psychiatry Review* 3, 69–175.

Fombonne, E., Wostear, G., Cooper, V., Harrington, R. and Rutter, M. (2001) 'The Maudsley long term follow up of child and adolescent depression 1 Psychiatric outcomes in adulthood', *British Journal of Psychiatry* 179, 218–223.

Fonagy, P., Target, M., Cottrell, D., Phillips, J. and Kurtz, Z. (2002) *What Works for Whom? A Critical Review of Treatments for Children and Adolescents.* London: Guilford Press.

Friedberg, R. and McClure, J. (2002) *Clinical Practice of Cognitive Therapy with Children and Adolescents. The Nuts and Bolts.* London: Guilford Press.

Geller, B., Cooper, T.B. and Sun, K. (1998) 'Double-blind and placebo controlled study of lithium for adolescent bipolar disorders with secondary substance dependency', *Journal of the American Academy of Child and Adolescent Psychiatry* 37, 171–178.

Goodman, R. (1997) 'The Strengths and Difficulties Questionnaire: a research note', *Journal of Child Psychology and Psychiatry* 38, 581–586.

Goodman, S.H. and Gotlib, I.H. (1999) 'Risk for psychopathology in the children of depressed mothers: a developmental model for understanding mechanisms of transmission', *Psychological Review* 106, 458–490.

Goodyer, I.M. and Cooper, P. (1993). 'A community study of depression in adolescent girls: II. The clinical features of identified disorder', *British Journal of Psychiatry* 163, 374–380.

Goodyer, I.M., Herbert, J. and Tamplin, A. (2003) 'Psychoendocrine antecedents of persistent first-episode major depression in adolescents: a community-based longitudinal enquiry', *Psychological Medicine* 33, 601–610.

Goodyer, I.M., Dubicka, B., Wilkinson, P., Kelvin, R., Roberts, C., Byford, S., Breen, S., Ford, C., Barrett, B., Leech, A., Rothwell, J., White, L. and Harrington, R. (2007) 'Selective serotonin inhibitors (SSRIs) and routine specialist care with and without cognitive behaviour therapy in adolescents with major depression: randomised controlled trial', *British Medical Journal* 335, 142–150.

Green, J. (2006) 'Annotation: The therapeutic alliance – a significant but neglected variable in child mental health treatment studies', *Journal of Child Psychology and Psychiatry* 47, 425–435.

Greenberger, D. and Padesky, C.A. (1995) *Mind over Mood. A Cognitive Therapy Treatment Manual for Clients.* New York: Guilford Press.

Hammen, C. (1991) *Depression Runs in Families. The Social Context of Risk and Resilience in Children of Depressed Mothers.* New York: Springer-Verlag.

Harrington, R.C. (1992) The natural history and treatment of child and adolescent affective disorders. *Journal of Child Psychology and Psychiatry* 33, 1287–1302.

Harrington, R. (1994) Affective disorders. In Rutter, M. and Hersov, L. (eds) *Child and Adolescent Psychiatry: Modern Methods*, 3rd edn (pp. 330–349). Oxford: Blackwell.

Harrington, R. (1999) Depressive disorders in children and adolescents. In Maj, M. and Sartorius, N. (eds) *Depressive Disorders* (pp. 233–265). London: John Wiley and Sons.

Harrington, R.C. and Dubicka, B. (2001) Natural history of mood disorders in children and adolescents. In Goodyer, I. (ed.) *The Depressed Child and Adolescent* (pp. 311–343). Cambridge: Cambridge University Press.

Harrington, R.C. and Wood, A. (1995) Validity and classification of child and adolescent depressive disorders. In Forrest, G. (ed.) *Childhood Depression. ACAMH Occasional Papers, 11*. London: ACAMH.

Harrington, R.C., Fudge, H., Rutter, M., Pickles, A. and Hill, J. (1991). 'Adult outcomes of childhood and adolescent depression: II. Risk for antisocial disorders', *Journal of the American Academy of Child and Adolescent Psychiatry* 30, 434–439.

Harrington, R.C., Rutter, M., Weissman, M., Fudge, H., Groothues, C., Bredenkamp, D., Rende, R., Pickles, A. and Wickramaratre, P. (1997) 'Psychiatric disorders in the relatives of depressed probands 1. Comparison of prepubertal, adolescent and early adult onset forms', *Journal of Affective Disorders* 42, 9–22.

Harter, S. (1985) *Manual for the Self Perception Profile for Children (revision of the Perceived Competence Scale for Children)*. Unpublished manuscript. University of Denver, Colorado.

Hawton, K. and Fagg, F. (1992) 'Deliberate self-poisoning and self-injury in adolescents. A study of characteristics and trends in Oxford, 1979–89', *British Journal of Psychiatry* 161, 816–823.

Hawton, K. and Rodham, K. (2006) *By Their Own Hand*. London: Jessica Kingsley Publishers.

Hazell, P., O'Connell, D., Heathcote, D., Robertson, J. and Henry, D. (1995) 'Efficacy of tricyclic drugs in treating child and adolescent depression: a meta analysis', *British Medical Journal* 310, 897–901.

Herbert, M. (1996) *Supporting Bereaved and Dying Children and their Parents*. Leicester: British Psychological Society.

Hill, K. (1995) *The Long Sleep. Young People and Suicide*. London: Virago Press.

Horowitz, M., Wilner, M. and Alvarez, W. (1979) Impact of Events scale-revised. In Wilson, J. and Keane, T. (eds) *Assessing Psychological Trauma and PTSD*. New York: Guilford.

Kaminer, D., Seedat, S. and Stein, D.J. (2005) 'Post-traumatic stress disorder in children', *World Psychiatry* 4, 121–5.

Kaslow, N.J., Stark, K.D., Printz, B., Livingston, R. and Tsai, S.L. (1992) 'Cognitive Triad Inventory for Children: development and relation to depression and anxiety', *Journal of Consulting and Clinical Psychology* 21, 339–347.

Kaufman, J., Birmaher, B., Brent, D., Rao, U., Flynn, C., Moreci, P., Williamson, D. and Ryan, N. (1997) 'Schedule for affective disorders and schizophrenia for school-age children-present and lifetime versions (K-SADS-PL): initial reliability and validity data', *Journal of the American Academy of Child and Adolescent Psychiatry* 36, 980–988.

Kazdin, A.E., French, N.H., Unis, A.S., Esvelat-Dawson, K. and Sherick, R.I. (1983) 'Hopelessness, depression & suicidal intent among psychiatrically disturbed inpatient children', *Journal of Consulting and Clinical Psychology* 51, 504–510.

Kendler, K.S., Kessler, R.C., Walters, E.E., MacLean, C., Neale, M.C., Heath, A.C. and Eaves, L.J. (1995) 'Stressful life events, genetic liability and onset of an episode of major depression in women', *American Journal of Psychiatry* 152, 833–842.

Kendler, K.S., Gardner, C.O. and Prescott, C.A. (2002) 'Towards a comprehensive developmental model for major depression in women', *American Journal of Psychiatry* 159, 1131–1145.

Kerfoot, M., Dyer, L., Harrington, V., Woodham, A. and Harrington, R. (1996) 'Correlates and short term course of self poisoning in adolescents', *British Journal of Psychiatry* 68, 38–42.

Khan, A., Khan, S., Khan, R. and Brown, W.A. (2003) 'Suicide rates in clinical trials of SSRIs, other antidepressants and placebo: analysis of FDA reports', *American Journal of Psychiatry* 160, 790–792.

Kirsch, I., Deacon, B., Huedo-Medina, T., Scoboria, A., Moore, T. and Johnson, B. (2008) 'Initial severity and antidepressant benefits: a meta-analysis of data submitted to the Food and Drug Administration', *PLOS Medicine* 5, 260–268.

Kovaacs, M. (1982) *The Children's Depression Inventory*. New York: Mental Health Systems.

Lewinsohn, P.M. and Clarke, G.N. (1999) 'Psychosocial treatments for adolescent depression', *Clinical Psychology Review* 19, 329–342.

Lewinsohn, P.M., Hoberman, H.M. and Clarke, G.N. (1989) 'The coping with depression course: review and future directions', *Canadian Journal of Behavioural Science* 21, 470–493.

March, J.S., Amaya-Jackson, L., Murray, M.C. and Schulte, A. (1998). 'Cognitive-behavioural psychotherapy for children and adolescents with post-traumatic stress disorder after a single-incident stressor', *Journal of the American Academy of Child and Adolescent Psychiatry* 37, 585–593.

Meiser-Stedman, R. (2002) 'Towards a cognitive-behavioral model of PTSD in children and adolescents', *Clinical Child and Family Psychology* 5, 217–232.

Meltzer, H., Gatward, R., Goodman, R. and Ford, T. (2000) *The Mental Health of Children and Adolescents in Great Britain*. London: The Stationery Office

Mental Health Foundation (1999) *The Big Picture, Promoting Children and Young People's Mental Health*. Presented at Young Minds conference, February 2002 in Liverpool.

Meyerson, L.A., Long, P.J. and Miranda, R.J. (2002) 'The influence of childhood sexual abuse, physical abuse, family environment and gender on the psychological adjustment of adolescents', *Child Abuse and Neglect* 26, 387–405.

Michael, K.D. and Crowley, S.L. (2002) 'How effective are treatments for child and adolescent depression?', *Clinical Psychology Review* 22, 247–269.

Miller, W.R. and Rollnik, S. (2002) *Motivational Interviewing: Preparing People for Change*, 2nd edn. New York: Guilford Press.

Mufson, L., Weissmann, M.M., Moreau, D. and Garfinkel, R. (1999) 'Efficacy of interpersonal psychotherapy for depressed adolescents', *Archives of General Psychiatry* 56, 573–579.

Mufson, L., Dorta, K., Wickramaratne, P., Nomura, Y., Olfson, M. and Weissman, M.M. (2004) 'A randomized effectiveness trial of interpersonal psychotherapy for depressed adolescents', *Archives of General Psychiatry* 61, 577–584.

Myers, W.H. (2000) 'A structural equation model of family factors associated with adolescent depression', *Dissertation Abstracts International: section B: The Sciences and Engineering* 61 (3B), 1620.

National Institute for Health and Clinical Excellence (2004) *Self Harm: The Short-Term Physical and Psychological Management and Secondary Prevention of Self Harm in Primary and Secondary Care*. Leicester: British Psychological Society.

National Institute for Health and Clinical Excellence (2005a) *Depression in Children and Young People: Identification and Management of Depression in Children and Young People in Primary, Community and Secondary Care.* Leicester: British Psychological Society.

National Institute for Health and Clinical Excellence (2005b) *The Management of Post Traumatic Stress Disorder in Adults and Children in Primary and Secondary Care.* Leicester: British Psychological Society.

National Institute for Health and Clinical Excellence (2009) *Personality Disorders: Borderline.* Leicester: British Psychological Society.

Ollendick, T.H. (1983) 'Reliability and validity of the Revised Fear Survey Schedule for Children (FSSC-R)', *Behaviour Research and Therapy* 21, 685–692.

Olsson, G.I. and Van Knorring, A.L. (1999) 'Adolescent depression: prevalence in Swedish high school students', *Acta Psychiatricia Scandinavica* 99, 324–331.

O'Moore, A.M., Kirkham, C. and Smith, M. (1997): 'Bullying behaviour in Irish schools: a nationwide study', *Irish Journal of Psychology* 18, 141–169.

Padesky, C.A. and Mooney, K.A. (1990) 'Presenting the cognitive behavioural model to clients', *International Cognitive Therapy Newsletter* 61, 13–14.

Pearce, J.B. (1978) 'The recognition of depressive disorder in children', *Journal of the Royal Society of Medicine* 71, 494–500.

Perrin, S., Smith, P. and Yule, W. (2000) 'Practitioner review: the assessment and treatment of post-traumatic disorder in children and adolescents', *Journal of Child Psychology and Psychiatry* 41, 277–289.

Pfeffer, C.R., Klerman, G.L., Hurt, S.W., Lesser, M., Peskin, J.R. and Siefker, C.A. (1991) 'Suicidal children grown up: demographic and clinical risk factors for adolescent suicidal attempts', *Journal of the American Academy of Child and Adolescent Psychiatry* 30, 609–616.

Pfeffer, C.R., Klerman, G.L., Hurt, S.W., Kakurma, T., Peskin, J.R. and Siefker, C.A. (1993) 'Suicidal children grown up and rates and psychological risk factors for attempts during follow-up', *Journal of the American Academy of Child and Adolescent Psychiatry* 32, 106–113.

Pfefferbaum, B. (1997) 'Post-traumatic stress disorder in children: a review of the past ten years', *Journal of the American Academy of Child and Adolescent Psychiatry* 36, 1503–1511.

Piers, E.V., Harris, D.B. and Herzberg, D.S. (2002) *Piers-Harris Self-Concept Scale,* 2nd edn. Los Angeles: Western Psychological Services.

Prochaska, J.O. and Diclemente, C.C. (1982) 'Transtheoretical therapy; towards a more integrative model of change', *Psychotherapy: Theory, Research and Practice* 19, 276–288.

Puig-Antich, J. (1982) 'Major depression and conduct disorder in prepuberty', *Journal of the American Academy of Child and Adolescent Psychiatry* 21, 118–128.

Puig-Antich, J. and Ryan, P. (1978) *Schedule for Affective Disorders and Schizophrenia for School Age Children (6–18 years)* (K-SADS). Unpublished manuscript. Pittsburgh PA: Western Psychiatric Institute and Clinic.

Quinton, D. and Rutter, M. (1985) Family pathology and psychiatric disorder. A four year prospective study. In Nicol, A. (ed.) *Longitudinal Studies in Child Psychology and Psychiatry.* Winchester: John Wiley.

Radke-Yarrow, M. (1998) *Children of Depressed Mothers.* Cambridge: Cambridge University Press.

Radke-Yarrow, M., Nottelmann, E., Martinez, P., Fox, M. and Belmont, B. (1992) 'Young children of affectively ill parents: a longitudinal study of psychosocial development', *Journal of the American Academy of Child and Adolescent Psychiatry* 31, 68–77.

Raphael, B., Middleton, W., Martinek, J. and Misso, V. (1993) Counselling and therapy of the bereaved. In Stroebe, M., Stroebe, W. and Hansson, R. (eds) *Handbook of Bereavement: Theory, Research and Intervention* (pp. 427–453). New York: Cambridge University Press.

Reich, W. (2000) 'Diagnostic Interview for Children and Adolescents (DICA)', *Journal of the American Academy of Child and Adolescent Psychiatry* 39, 59–66.

Reinecke, M.A., Ryan, N.E. and Dubois, D.L. (1998) 'Cognitive-behavioral therapy of depression and depressive symptoms in adolescence', *Journal of the American Academy of Child and Adolescent Psychiatry*, 37, 26–34.

Reynolds, W.M. and Richmond, B.O. (1985) *Revised Children's Manifest Anxiety Scale* (RCMAS). Los Angeles: Western Psychological Services.

Roberts, R.E., Roberts, C.R. and Chen, Y.R. (1997) 'Ethnocultural differences prevalence of adolescent depression', *American Journal of Community Psychology* 25, (1): 95–100.

Rossello, J. and Bernal, G. (1999) 'The efficacy of cognitive behavioural and interpersonal treatments for depression in Puerto Rican adolescents', *Journal of Consulting and Clinical Psychology* 67, 734–745.

Ryan, N.D., Puig-Antich, J., Ambrosini, P., Rabinovich, H., Robinson, D., Nelson, B., Iyengar, S. and Twomey, J. (1987) 'The clinical picture of major depression in childhood and adolescence', *Archives of General Psychiatry* 44, 854–861.

Seligman, M.E.P. (1975) *Helplessness: On Depression, Development and Death*. San Francisco CA: Freeman.

Shaffer, D. and Craft, L. (1999) 'Methods of adolescent suicide prevention', *Journal of Clinical Psychiatry* 60 (suppl 2): 70–4; discussion 95–96, 113–116.

Shaffer, D. and Piacentini, J. (1994) Suicide and attempted suicide. In Rutter, M., Taylor, E. and Hersov, L. (eds) *Child and Adolescent Psychiatry: Modern Approaches*, 3rd edn (pp. 407–424). Oxford: Blackwell.

Shirk, S.R. (2002) *The Therapeutic Relationship and Outcome in Child and Adolescent Therapy*. Paper presented at International Congress of Psychotherapy, Trondheim, Norway.

Shirk, S.R. and Karver, M. (2003) 'Prediction of treatment outcome from relationship variables in child and adolescent therapy: a meta-analytic review', *Journal of Consulting and Clinical Psychology* 71, 452–464.

Silverman, P. and Worden, J. (1993). Children's reaction to the death of a parent. In Stroeke, M., Stroebe, W. and Hansson, R. (eds) *Handbook of Bereavement: Theory, Research and Intervention* (pp. 300–316). New York: Cambridge University Press.

Simmons, J., Cooper, M.J., Drinkwater, J. and Stewart, A. (2006) 'Cognitive schemata in depressed adolescent girls and their mothers', *Behavioural and Cognitive Psychotherapy* 34, 219–232.

Smith, P.K., Cowie, H. and Sharp, S. (1994) Working directly with pupils involved in bullying situation. In Smith, P.K. and Sharp, S. (eds) *School Bullying: Insights and Perspectives*. London: Routledge.

Smith, P., Perrin, S., Yule, W. and Rabe-Hesketh, S. (2001) 'War exposure and maternal reactions in the psychological adjustment of children from Bosnia-Hercegovina', *Journal of Child Psychology and Psychiatry* 42, 395–404.

Spence, S.H. (2005) *Enhancing Social Competence with Children and Adolescents*. London: NFER-Nelson.

Spielberger, C.D., Edwards, C.D., Lushene, R., Montuori, D. and Platzek, D. (1983)

State-Trait Anxiety Inventory for Children (STAI-C). Lutz, Florida: Psychological Assessment Resources.

Spiker, D.G., Weiss, J.C., Dealy, R.S., Griffin, S.J., Hanin, I., Neil, J.F., Perel, J.M., Rossi, A.J. and Soloff, P.H. (1985) 'The pharmaceutical treatment of delusional depression', *American Journal of Psychiatry* 142, 430–436.

Stallard, P. (2002) 'Cognitive behaviour therapy with children and young people; a selective review of key issues', *Behavioural and Cognitive Psychotherapy* 30, 297–309.

Stallard, P. and Rayner, H. (2005) 'The development and preliminary evaluation of a schema questionnaire for children (SQC)', *Behavioural and Cognitive Psychotherapy* 33, 217–22.

Stallard, P., Velleman, R. and Baldwin, S. (1998) 'Prospective study of post-traumatic stress disorder in children involved in road traffic accidents', *British Medical Journal* 317, 1619–1632.

Stark, K.D. (1990). *Childhood Depression: School-based Intervention*. New York: Guilford.

Stark, K.D., Best, L.R. and Adam, T. (1990) *Development and Psychometric Evaluation of a Depressogenic Thought Questionnaire for Children*. Unpublished manuscript.

Taylor, E.A. and Stansfield, S.A. (1984) 'Children who poison themselves: a clinical comparison with psychiatric controls', *British Journal of Psychiatry* 145, 127–32.

Thabet, A.A., Abed, Y. and Vostanis, P. (2004) 'Comorbidity of PTSD and depression among refugee children during war conflict', *Journal of Child Psychology and Psychiatry* 45, 533–542.

Thompson, M. and Gauntlett-Gilbert, J. (2008) 'Mindfulness with children and adolescents: effective clinical application', *Clinical Child Psychology and Psychiatry* 13, 395–407.

Thompson, M., Kaslow, N., Weiss, B. and Nolen-Hoeksma, S. (1998) 'Children's Attributional Style Questionnaire (CASQ-R)' *Psychological Assessment* 10, 166–170.

Tousignant, M., Habimana, E., Biron, C., Malo, C., Sidoli–LeBlanc, E. and Bendris, N. (1999). 'The Quebec adolescent refugee project: Psychopathology and family variables in a sample from 35 nations', *Journal of the American Academy of Child and Adolescent Psychiatry* 38, 1426–1432.

Treatment for Adolescents with Depression (TADS) (2004) 'Fluoxetine, cognitive behavioral therapy and their combination for adolescents with depression: Treatment for Adolescents with Depression (TADS) randomized controlled trial', *Journal of the American Medical Association* 292, 807–820.

Treatment for Adolescents with Depression (TADS) (2007) 'The Treatment for Adolescents with Depression Study (TADS) Long term effectiveness and safety outcomes', *Archives of General Psychiatry* 64, 1132–1144.

Trowell, J., Joffe, I., Campbell, J., Clemente, C., Almqvist, F., Soininen, M., Koskenranta-Aalto, U., Weintraub, S., Kolaitis, G., Tomaras, V., Anastasopoulos, D., Grayson, K., Barnes, J. and Tsiantis, J. (2007) 'Childhood depression: a place for psychotherapy. An outcome study comparing individual psychodynamic psychotherapy and family therapy', *European Child and Adolescent Psychiatry* 16, 157–167.

Tsapakis, E., Soldani, F., Tondo, L. and Baldessarini, J. (2008) 'Efficacy of antidepressants in juvenile depression: meta-analysis', *British Journal of Psychiatry* 19, 10–17.

Watanabe, N., Hunot, V., Omori, I.M., Churchill, R. and Furukawa, T.A. (2007)

'Psychotherapy for depression among children and adolescents: a systematic review', *Acta Psychiatrica Scandinavica* 116, 84–95.

Weinberg, W.A., Rutman, J., Sullivan, L., Penick, E.C. and Dietz, S.G. (1973) 'Depression in children referred to an educational diagnostic centre; diagnosis and treatment', *Journal of Paediatrics* 83, 1065–1072.

Weissman, M., Wolks, M., Goldstein, R.B., Moreau, D., Adams, P., Greenwald, S., Klier, C.M., Ryan, N.D., Dahl, R.E. and Wickramaratne, P. (1999) 'Depressed adolescents grow up', *Journal of the American Medical Association* 281, 1701–1713.

Weisz, J.R., McCarty, C.A. and Valeri, S.M. (2006) 'Effects of psychotherapy for depression in children and adolescents a meta-analysis', *Psychological Bulletin* 132, 132–149.

Whitney, I. and Smith, P.K. (1993) 'A survey of the nature and extent of bullying in junior/middle and secondary schools', *Education Research* 35, 3–25.

Wilkes, T.C.R., Belsher, G., Rush, A.J. and Frank, E. (1994) *Cognitive Therapy for Depressed Adolescents.* London: Guilford Press.

Wolfe, V.V. and Wolfe, D.A. (1986) *The Sexual Abuse Fear Evaluation (SAFE): A Subscale for the Fear Survey Schedule for Children – Revised.* Unpublished questionnaire. University of Western Ontario, London, Ontario.

Wolfe, V.V., Gentile, C., Michienzi, T., Sas, L. and Wolfe, D.A. (1991) 'The Childrens Impact of Traumatic Events scale: a measure of post-sexual abuse PTSD symptoms', *Behaviour Assessment* 13, 159–383.

Wolpert, M., Doe, J. and Elsworth, J. (2005) Working with parents: ethical and practical issues. In Graham, P. (ed.) *CBT for Children and Families*, 2nd edn. Cambridge: Cambridge University Press.

World Health Organization (1993) *The ICD-10 Classification of Mental and Behavioural Disorders: Diagnostic Criteria for Research.* Geneva: World Health Organization.

Young, J. (1998) *The Young Schema Questionnaire – Shortened Inventory.* (www.schematherapy.com).

Yule, W., Bolton, D., Udwin, O., Boyle, S., O'Ryan, D. and Nurrish, J. (2000) 'The long-term psychological effects of a disaster experienced in adolescence. I The incidence and course of PTSD', *Journal of Child Psychology and Psychiatry* 41, 503–511.

Index

Note: References to materials and worksheets are in *italic*; those to figures are as 50*f*.